INSPIRE MATHS

PUPIL TEXTBOOK 4B

Consultant and author
Dr Fong Ho Kheong

Authors
Chelvi Ramakrishnan and Gan Kee Soon

UK consultants
Carole Skinner, Simon d'Angelo and Elizabeth Gibbs

Published by Marshall Cavendish Education
Times Centre, 1 New Industrial Road, Singapore 536196
Customer Service Hotline: (65) 6213 9444
Email: tmesales@mceducation.com
Website: www.mceducation.com

Distributed by
Oxford University Press
Great Clarendon Street, Oxford,
OX2 6DP, United Kingdom
www.oxfordprimary.co.uk
www.oxfordowl.co.uk

First published 2015
Reprinted 2015

ISBN 978-981-01-8888-7

Printed in China

Acknowledgements
Written by Dr Fong Ho Kheong, Chelvi Ramakrishnan and Gan Kee Soon

UK consultants: Carole Skinner, Simon d'Angelo and Elizabeth Gibbs

Cover artwork by Daron Parton

The authors and publisher would like to thank all schools and individuals who helped to trial and review Inspire Maths resources.

Introduction

Inspire Maths is a comprehensive, activity-based programme designed to provide pupils with a firm foundation in maths and to develop the creative and critical thinking skills to become fluent problem solvers.

Inspire Maths makes learning maths fun and rewarding through the use of engaging illustrations and games that help to reinforce and consolidate learning.

For the teacher:

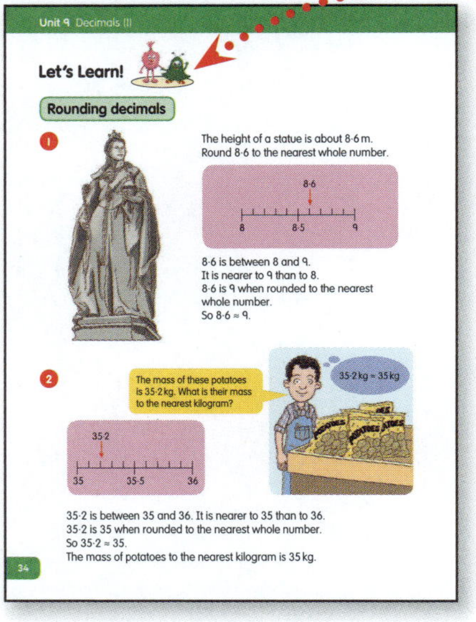
Unit 9 Decimals (1)

Let's Learn!

Rounding decimals

1 The height of a statue is about 8·6 m.
Round 8·6 to the nearest whole number.

8·6 is between 8 and 9.
It is nearer to 9 than to 8.
8·6 is 9 when rounded to the nearest whole number.
So 8·6 ≈ 9.

2 The mass of these potatoes is 35·2 kg. What is their mass to the nearest kilogram?

35·2 kg ≈ 35 kg

35·2 is between 35 and 36. It is nearer to 35 than to 36.
35·2 is 35 when rounded to the nearest whole number.
So 35·2 ≈ 35.
The mass of potatoes to the nearest kilogram is 35 kg.

34

Use the engaging and highly scaffolded **Let's Learn!** to introduce concepts. Integrated questions allow for immediate assessment and consolidation of concepts learnt.

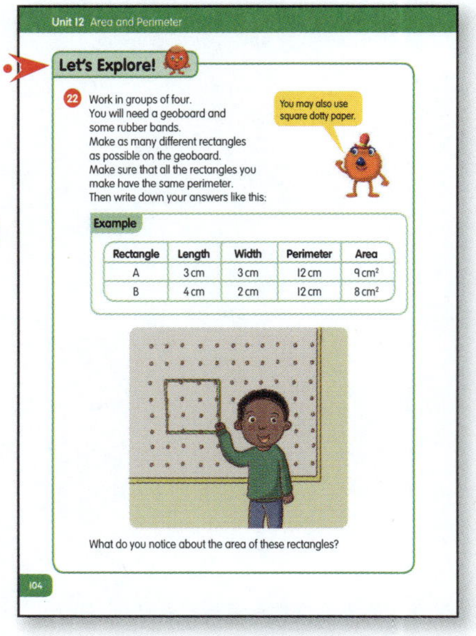
Unit 12 Area and Perimeter

Let's Explore!

22 Work in groups of four.
You will need a geoboard and some rubber bands.
Make as many different rectangles as possible on the geoboard.
Make sure that all the rectangles you make have the same perimeter.
Then write down your answers like this:

You may also use square dotty paper.

Example

Rectangle	Length	Width	Perimeter	Area
A	3 cm	3 cm	12 cm	9 cm²
B	4 cm	2 cm	12 cm	8 cm²

What do you notice about the area of these rectangles?

104

Carry out investigative activities in **Let's Explore!** These allow pupils to apply concepts learnt.

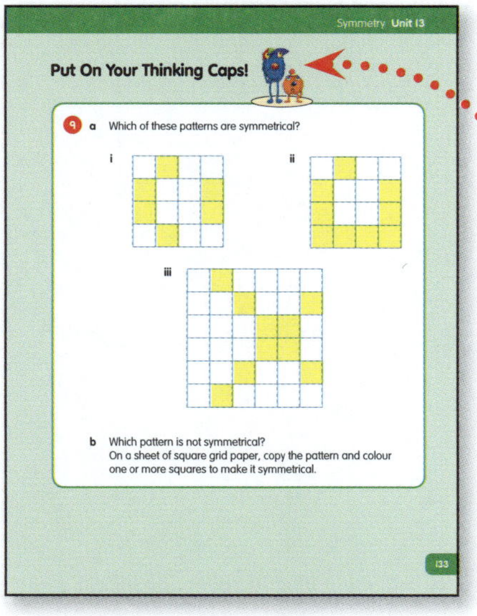
Symmetry Unit 13

Put On Your Thinking Caps!

9 a Which of these patterns are symmetrical?
i ii iii

b Which pattern is not symmetrical?
On a sheet of square grid paper, copy the pattern and colour one or more squares to make it symmetrical.

133

Challenge pupils to solve non-routine questions by applying relevant heuristics and thinking skills in **Put On Your Thinking Caps!**

For the parent/guardian:

Home Maths

Build home-school links and make maths come alive by using the tips in Home Maths to help children apply mathematical concepts to daily life.

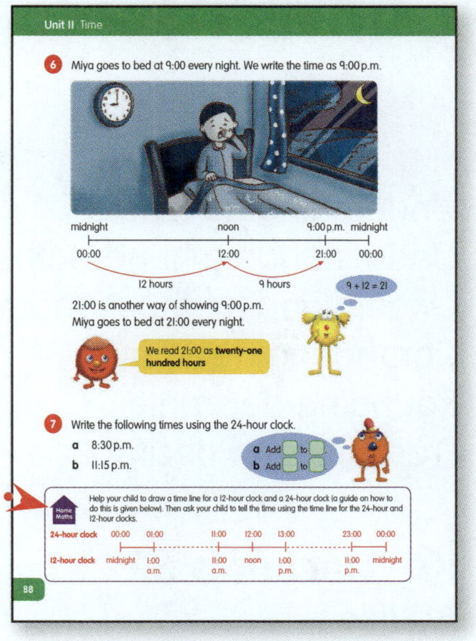
Unit 11 Time

6 Miya goes to bed at 9:00 every night. We write the time as 9:00 p.m.

21:00 is another way of showing 9:00 p.m.
Miya goes to bed at 21:00 every night.

We read 21:00 as twenty-one hundred hours

7 Write the following times using the 24-hour clock.

a 8:30 p.m.
b 11:15 p.m.

a Add ☐ to ☐
b Add ☐ to ☐

Home Maths: Help your child to draw a time line for a 12-hour clock and a 24-hour clock (a guide on how to do this is given below). Then ask your child to tell the time using the time line for the 24-hour and 12-hour clocks.

24-hour clock	00:00	01:00	11:00	12:00	13:00	23:00	00:00
12-hour clock	midnight	1:00 a.m.	11:00 a.m.	noon	1:00 p.m.	11:00 p.m.	midnight

88

For the pupil:

Enjoy **Inspire Maths** with your friends. Explore your learning through activities and games.

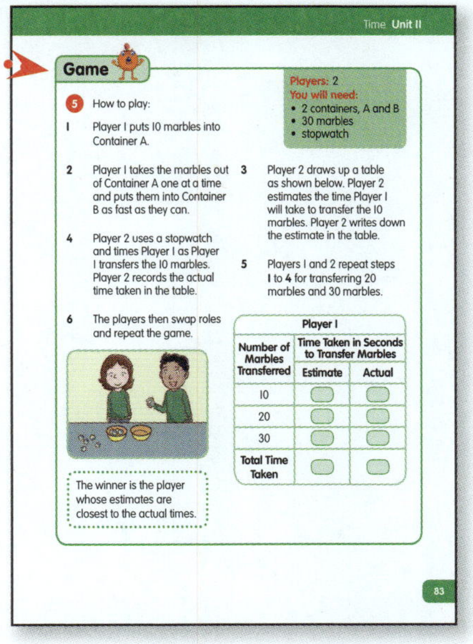
Time Unit 11

Game

Players: 2
You will need:
- 2 containers, A and B
- 30 marbles
- stopwatch

5 How to play:

1 Player 1 puts 10 marbles into Container A.

2 Player 1 takes the marbles out of Container A one at a time and puts them into Container B as fast as they can.

3 Player 2 draws up a table as shown below. Player 2 estimates the time Player 1 will take to transfer the 10 marbles. Player 2 writes down the estimate in the table.

4 Player 2 uses a stopwatch and times Player 1 as Player 1 transfers the 10 marbles. Player 2 records the actual time taken in the table.

5 Players 1 and 2 repeat steps 1 to 4 for transferring 20 marbles and 30 marbles.

6 The players then swap roles and repeat the game.

Player 1

Number of Marbles Transferred	Time Taken in Seconds to Transfer Marbles	
	Estimate	Actual
10	☐	☐
20	☐	☐
30	☐	☐
Total Time Taken	☐	☐

The winner is the player whose estimates are closest to the actual times.

83

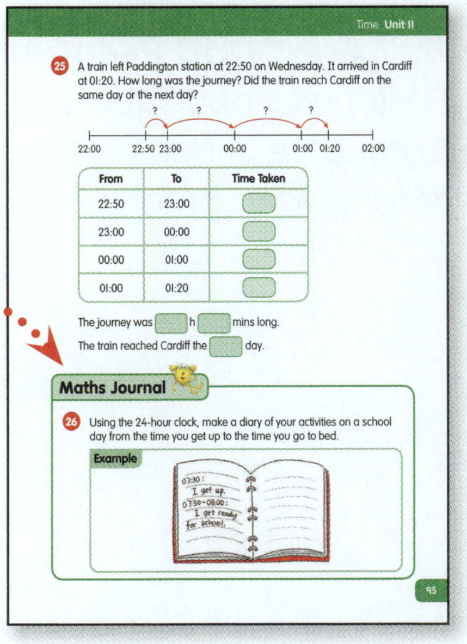
Time Unit 11

25 A train left Paddington station at 22:50 on Wednesday. It arrived in Cardiff at 01:20. How long was the journey? Did the train reach Cardiff on the same day or the next day?

From	To	Time Taken
22:50	23:00	☐
23:00	00:00	☐
00:00	01:00	☐
01:00	01:20	☐

The journey was ☐ h ☐ mins long.
The train reached Cardiff the ☐ day.

Maths Journal

26 Using the 24-hour clock, make a diary of your activities on a school day from the time you get up to the time you go to bed.

Example

95

Share what you have learnt, create your own questions and become aware of your own mathematical thinking in your **Maths Journal**.

Contents

Unit 9

Decimals (I)

Let's Learn!

Understanding tenths

1

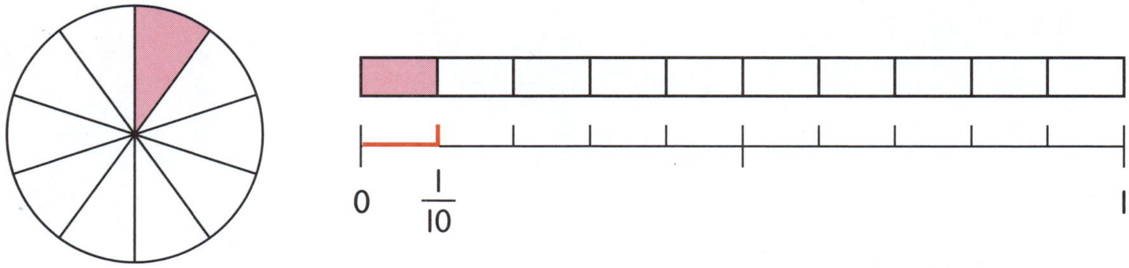

Each whole is divided into ten equal parts.

Each part is $\frac{1}{10}$ **(one-tenth)**.

We write $\frac{1}{10}$ as **0·1** as a decimal.

0·1 is 1 tenth written as a decimal.

> 0·1
> ↑
> decimal point
>
> We read 0·1 as **zero point one**.
> Its value is 1 tenth.

2

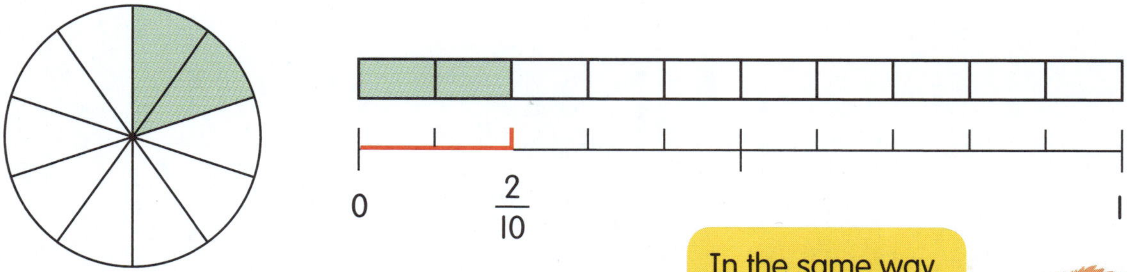

Two parts is $\frac{2}{10}$ (two-tenths).

We write $\frac{2}{10}$ as 0·2 as a decimal.

In the same way, I write $\frac{3}{10}$ as 0·3 and $\frac{4}{10}$ as 0·4.

3 What is the decimal for each of the following?

a $\frac{5}{10}$ = ☐

b $\frac{6}{10}$ = ☐

c 3 tenths = ☐

d 8 tenths = ☐

4 What decimals do the following shaded and unshaded parts represent?

a

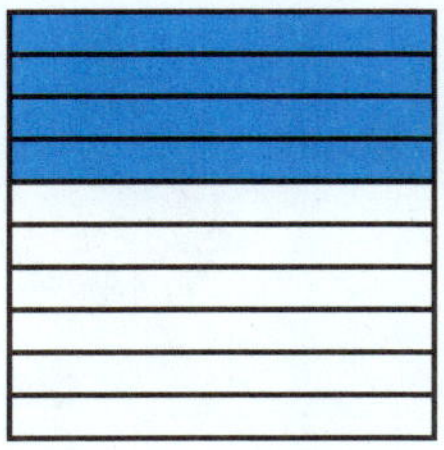

shaded parts = ☐

unshaded parts = ☐

b

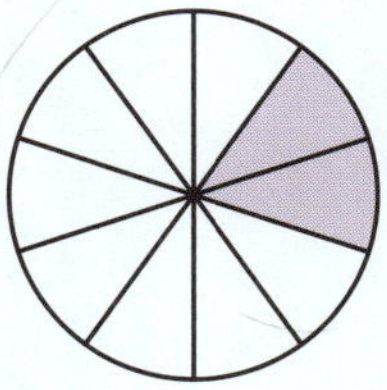

shaded parts = ☐

unshaded parts = ☐

5 What is the decimal for each point on the number line?

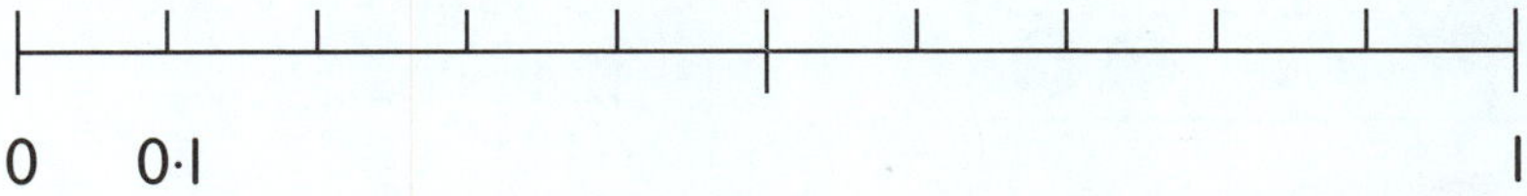

6

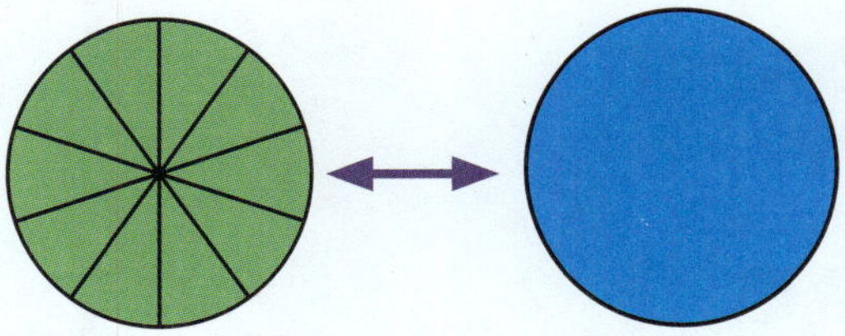

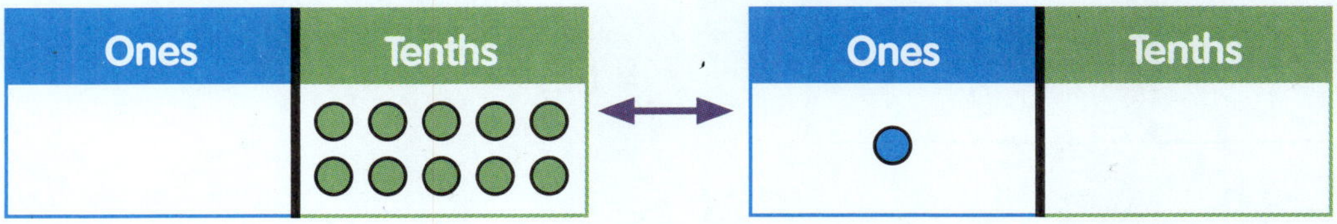

$\frac{10}{10}$ is equal to 1.

10 tenths = 1 one

You can exchange 10 tenths for 1 one.

7 Change $1\frac{6}{10}$ to a decimal.

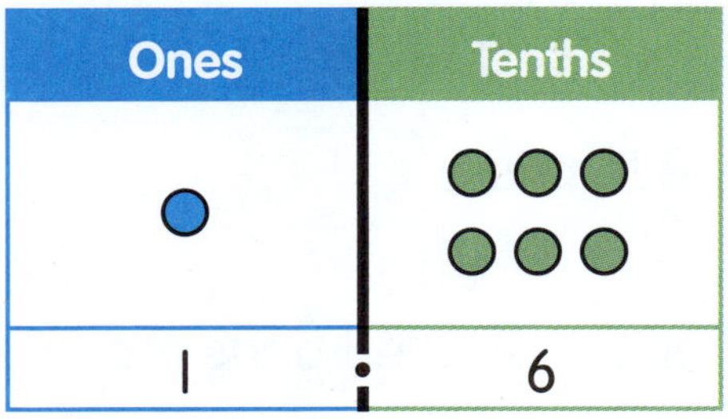

$1\frac{6}{10}$ = 1 one 6 tenths

= 1·6

We read 1·6 as **one point six.**

8 Change $\frac{12}{10}$ to a decimal.

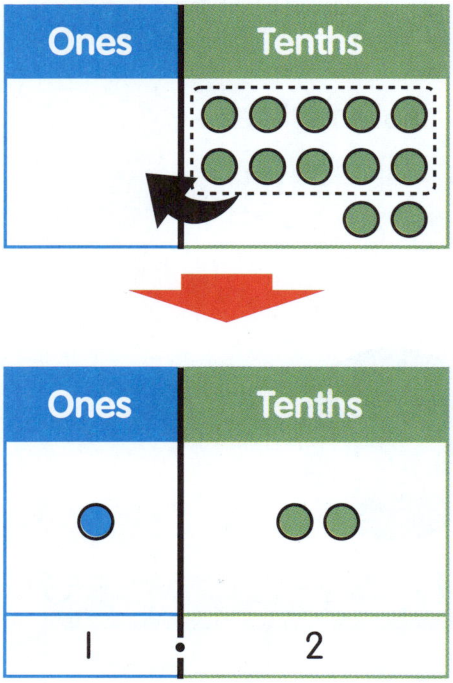

$\frac{12}{10}$ = 12 tenths

10 tenths = 1 one

12 tenths

1 one   2 tenths

$\frac{12}{10}$ = 1 one 2 tenths

= 1·2

9 What is the decimal for each of the following?

a 15 tenths = ☐

b 2 ones 3 tenths = ☐

10 What decimals do the following shaded parts represent?

a

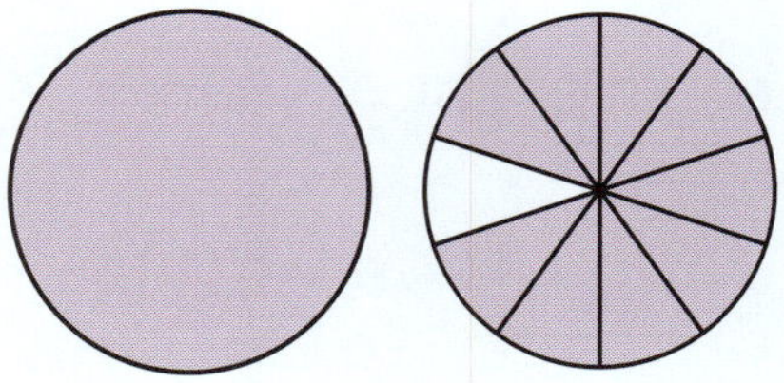

shaded parts = ☐

b

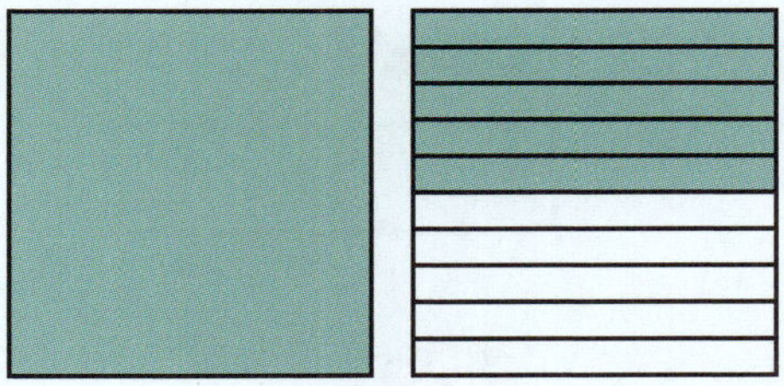

shaded parts = ☐

11 Look at the points marked with a cross (X) on the number line.
What decimals do these points represent?

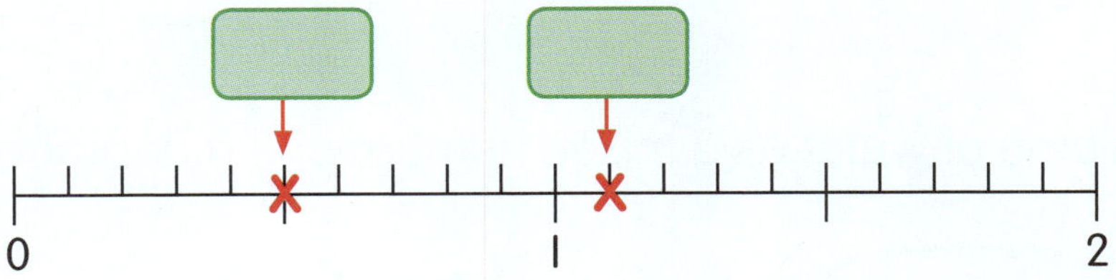

12 What is the decimal for each of the following?

a

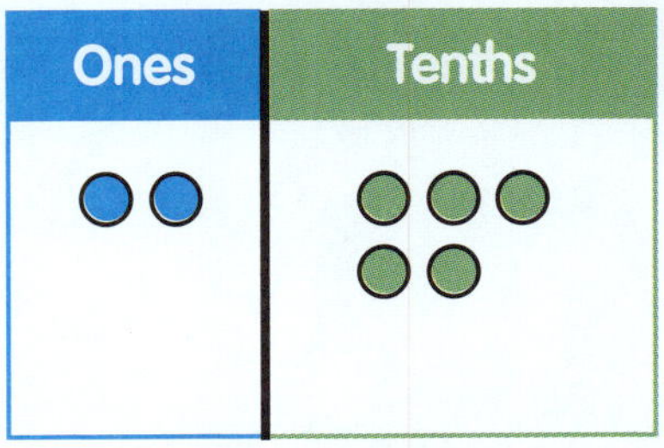

☐

b

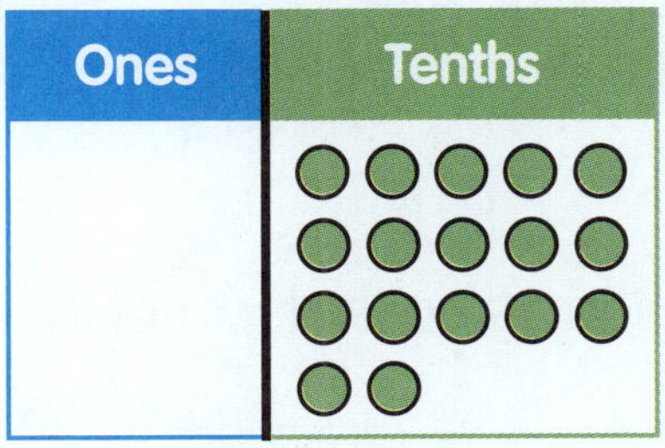

☐

c $2\frac{9}{10}$ = ☐

d $\frac{27}{10}$ = ☐

13 Express the length of each insect as a fraction and a decimal.

a

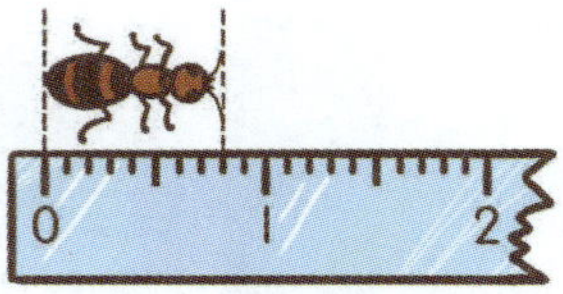

Length of ant $= \frac{8}{10}$ cm

$= 0{\cdot}8$ cm

b

Length of ladybird = ____ cm

= ____ cm

c

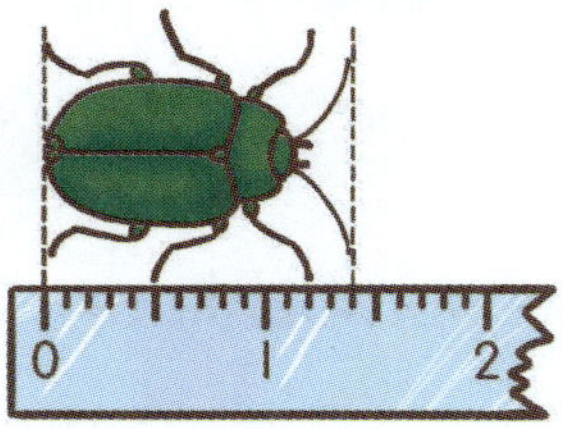

Length of beetle = ____ cm

= ____ cm

14 Express the total volume of water as a mixed number and a decimal.

Total volume of water $= 1\frac{\square}{\square}$ ℓ

= ____ ℓ

15 What is each decimal in tenths?

a 0·2 = ____

b 0·7 = ____

c 1·1 = ____

d 1·3 = ____

16

Tens	Ones	Tenths
4	2	3

$42{\cdot}3 = 4$ tens 2 ones 3 tenths

$= 40 + 2 + 0{\cdot}3$

$= 40 + 2 + \frac{3}{10}$

17 Find the missing numbers.

$76{\cdot}4 =$ ☐ tens ☐ ones ☐ tenths

$= 70 + 6 +$ ☐

$= 70 + 6 + \frac{☐}{10}$

18 In 23·6:

the digit 2 is in the tens place.
the digit 3 stands for 3 ones or 3.
the value of the digit 6 is 0·6.

19 Find the missing numbers.

a In 49·8, the digit ☐ is in the tenths place.

b In 95·6, the digit 5 stands for ☐.

c In 50·2, the value of the digit 0 is ☐.

d In 92·9, the digit 9 stands for ☐ and ☐.

Home Maths

Encourage your child to point out decimal numbers when you go shopping together. Decimals can be found in the nutrition information on food labels, on price labels, on digital weighing scales and in many other places.

Practice Book 4B, p.7

Let's Learn!

Understanding hundredths

1

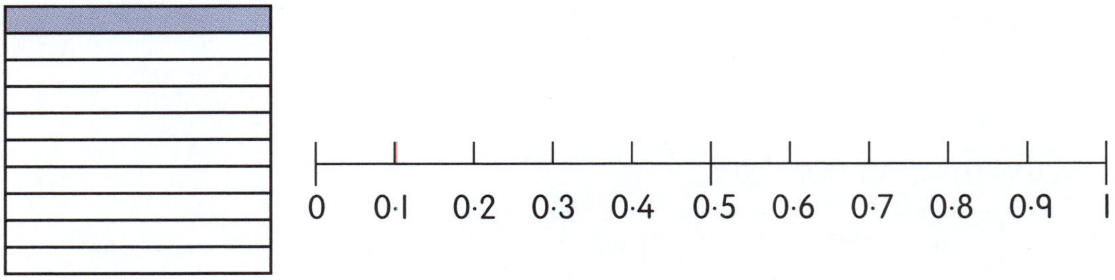

The square and the number line are each divided into ten equal parts.
Each part is 1 tenth.

Divide each tenth into ten equal parts.
Now the square and the number line each have 100 equal parts.

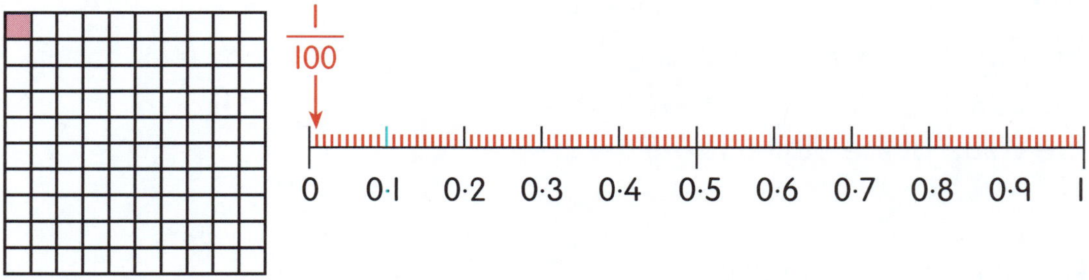

Each part is $\frac{1}{100}$ **(one hundredth)**.

We write $\frac{1}{100}$ as **0·01** as a decimal form.

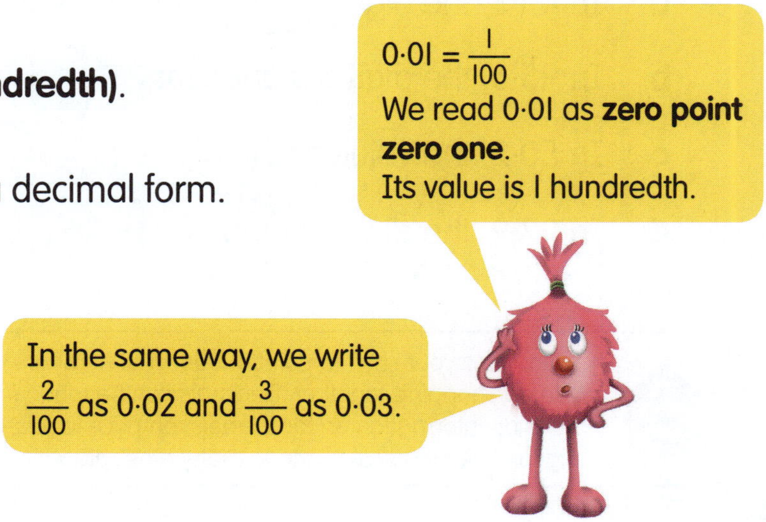

2 What is the decimal for each of the following?

a $\frac{4}{100}$ g = [ ] g

b $\frac{6}{100}$ cm = [ ] cm

c 7 hundredths = [ ]

d 8 hundredths = [ ]

3 What decimals do the following shaded parts represent?

a

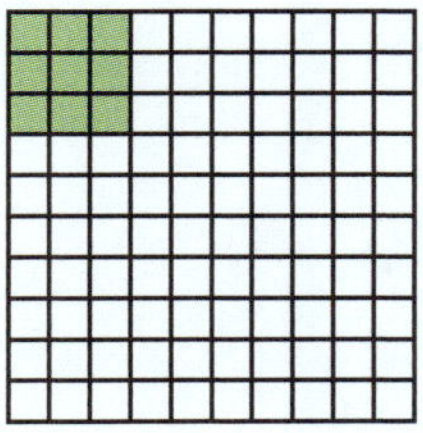

shaded parts = [ ]

b

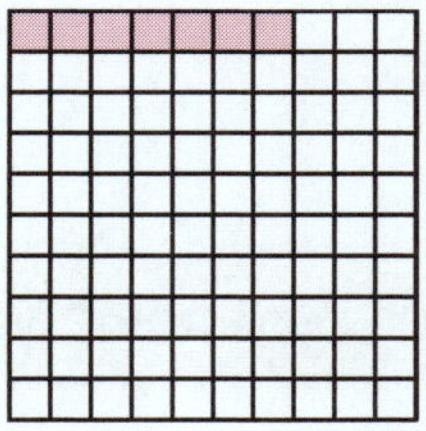

shaded parts = [ ]

4 What is the decimal for each point on the number line?

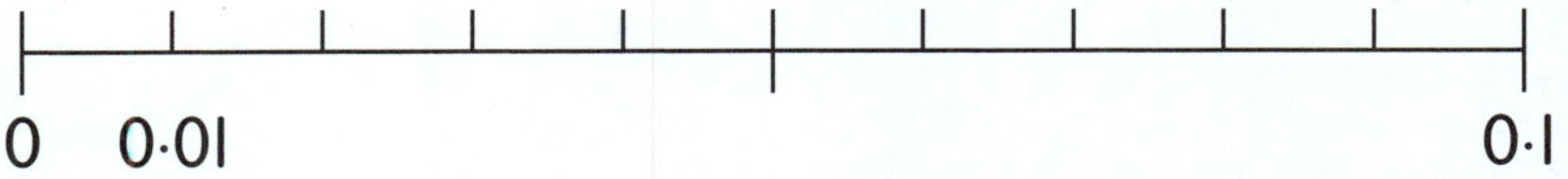

5

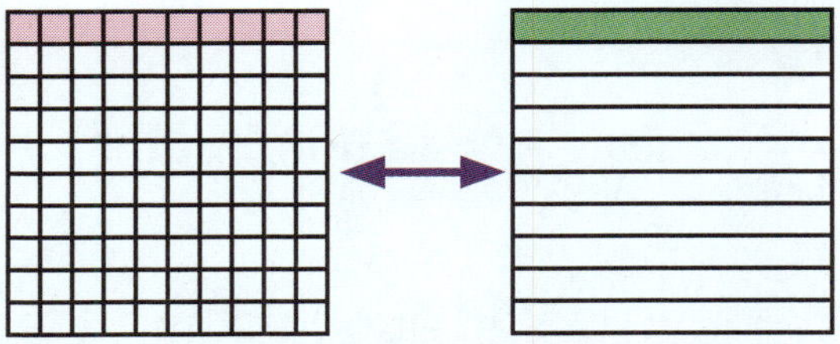

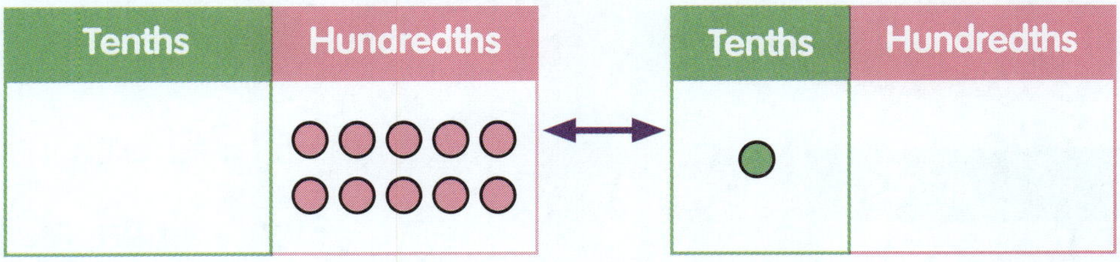

$\frac{10}{100}$ is equal to $\frac{1}{10}$ or 0·1.

10 hundredths = 1 tenth

You can exchange 10 hundredths for 1 tenth.

6 What is 2 tenths 5 hundredths written as a decimal?

Ones	Tenths	Hundredths
0 ·	2	5

2 tenths 5 hundredths = 0·25

We read 0·25 as **zero point two five**.

7 Change $\frac{15}{100}$ to a decimal.

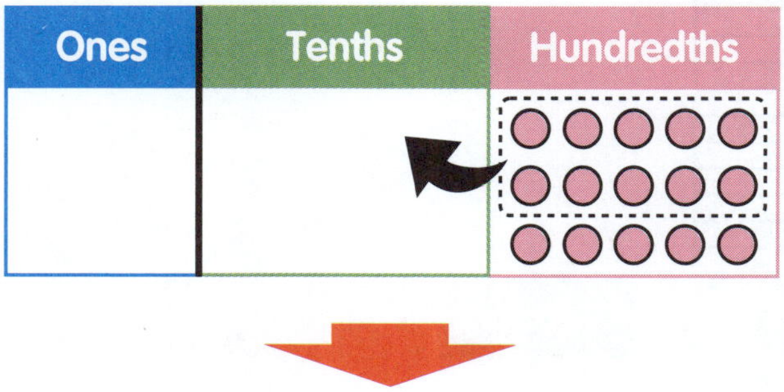

Ones	Tenths	Hundredths
0 ·	1	5

$\frac{15}{100}$ = 15 hundredths

10 hundredths = 1 tenth

15 hundredths

1 tenth 5 hundredths

$\frac{15}{100}$ = 1 tenth 5 hundredths

= 0·15

8 What decimals do the following shaded parts represent?

a

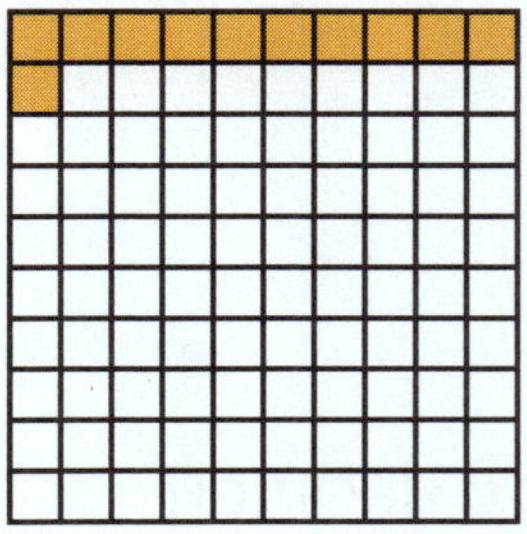

shaded parts = ☐

b

shaded parts = ☐

9 Look at the points marked with a cross (X) on the number line.
What decimals do these points represent?

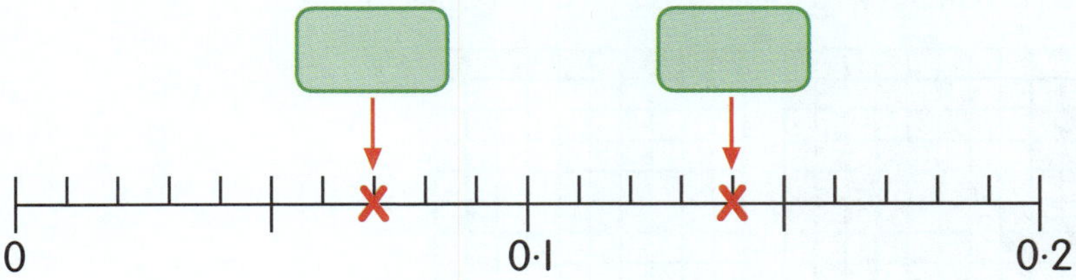

10 What is the decimal for each of the following?

a

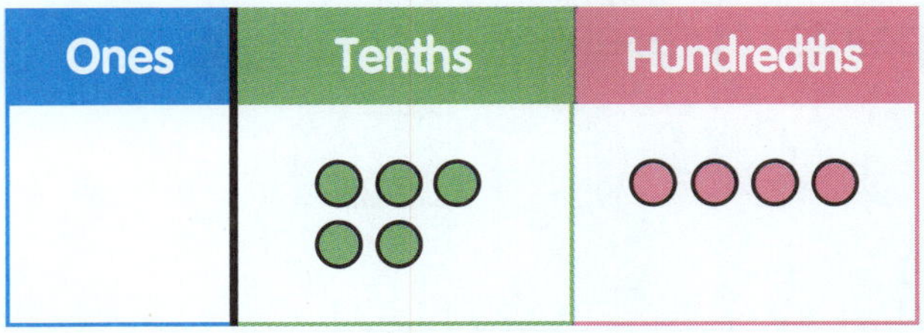

☐

b

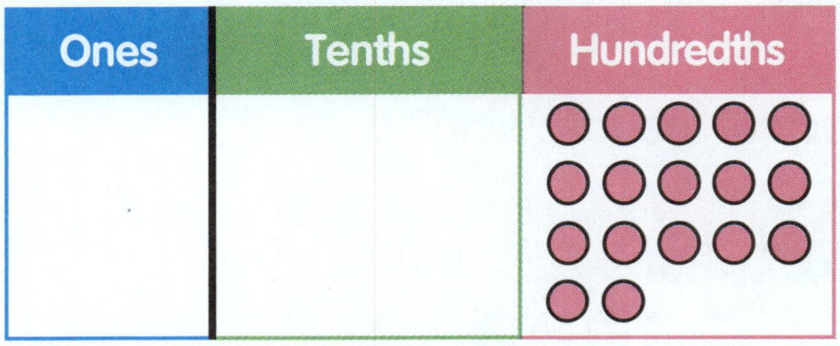

☐

c $\frac{21}{100}$ = ☐

d $\frac{87}{100}$ = ☐

11 Does 0·9 have the same value as 0·90?

$0{\cdot}90 = \frac{90}{100}$

$= \frac{9}{10}$

$= 0{\cdot}9$

12 What is 2 ones 4 tenths 7 hundredths written as a decimal?

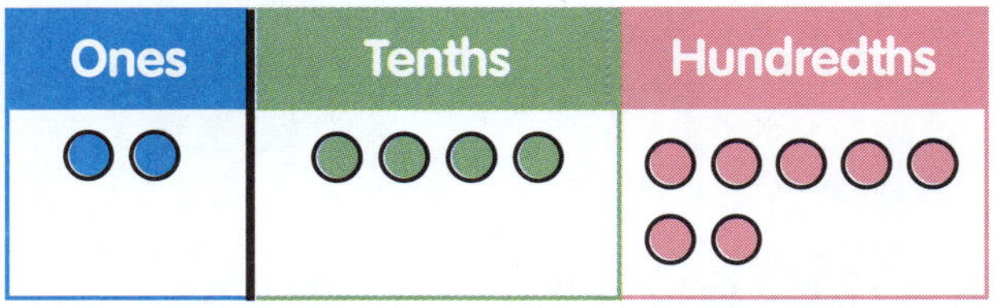

13 What decimal do the following shaded parts represent?

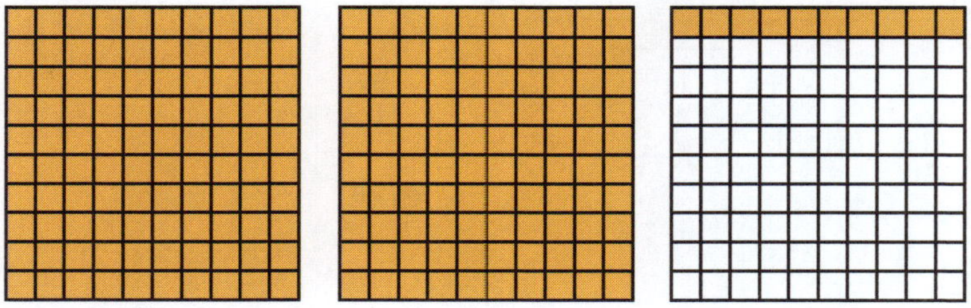

shaded parts =

14 Look at the points marked with a cross (X) on the number line.
What decimals do these points represent?

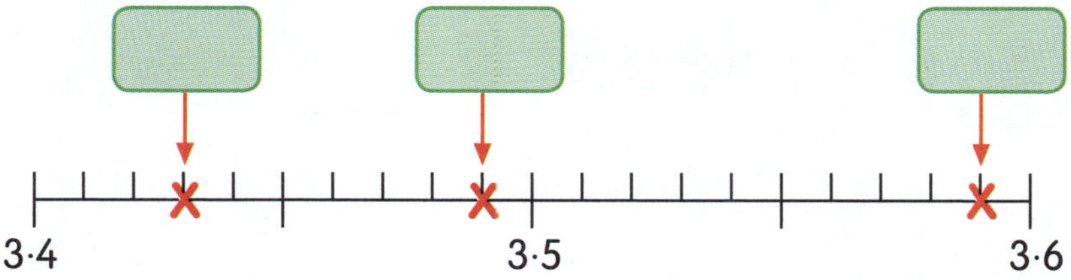

15 What is the decimal for each of the following?

a

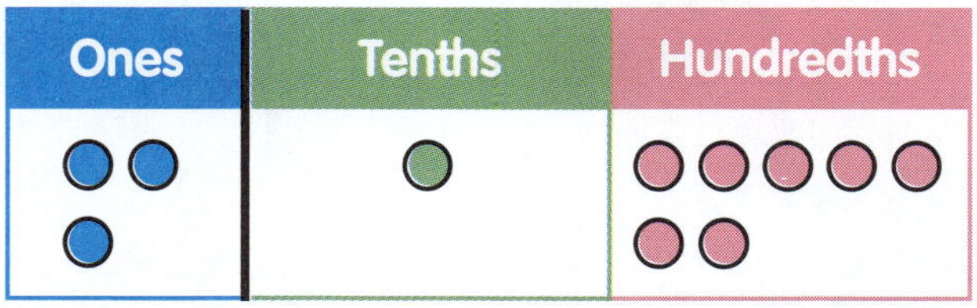

b 4 ones 9 tenths 1 hundredth =

16 Change $1\frac{53}{100}$ to a decimal.

Ones	Tenths	Hundredths
●	●●●●●	●●●
1 •	5	3

$1\frac{53}{100}$ = 1 one 5 tenths 3 hundredths
= 1·53

17 Change $\frac{147}{100}$ to a decimal.

$\frac{147}{100}$ = 147 hundredths

100 hundredths = 1 one

147 hundredths

1 one   47 hundredths

$\frac{147}{100}$ = 1 one 47 hundredths
= 1·47

18 What is the decimal for each of the following?

a $2\frac{75}{100}$ = ☐

b $\frac{103}{100}$ = ☐

c $3\frac{16}{100}\ell$ = ☐ ℓ

d $\frac{204}{100}$ km = ☐ km

19 What is each decimal in hundredths?

a 0·02 = ☐

b 0·31 = ☐

c 2·05 = ☐

20

Tens	Ones	Tenths	Hundredths
7	8 •	4	1

78·41 = 7 tens 8 ones 4 tenths 1 hundredth
= 70 + 8 + 0·4 + 0·01
= $70 + 8 + \frac{4}{10} + \frac{1}{100}$

21 Find the missing numbers.

20·39 = ____ tens ____ ones ____ tenths ____ hundredths

= 20 + 0·3 + ____

$= 20 + \frac{\square}{10} + \frac{\square}{100}$

22 In 3·47:

the digit 3 is in the ones place.
the digit 4 stands for 4 tenths or 0·4.
the value of the digit 7 is 0·07.

23 Answer these questions.

a In 5·18, the digit 1 is in the ____ place.

b In 2·59, the digit 9 stands for ____.

c In 82·03, the value of the digit 8 is ____.

24

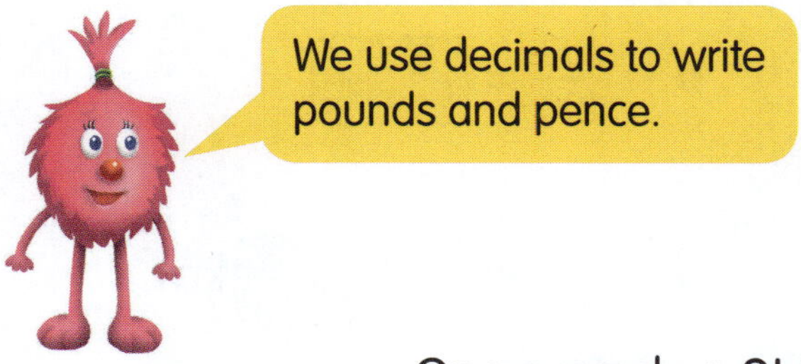

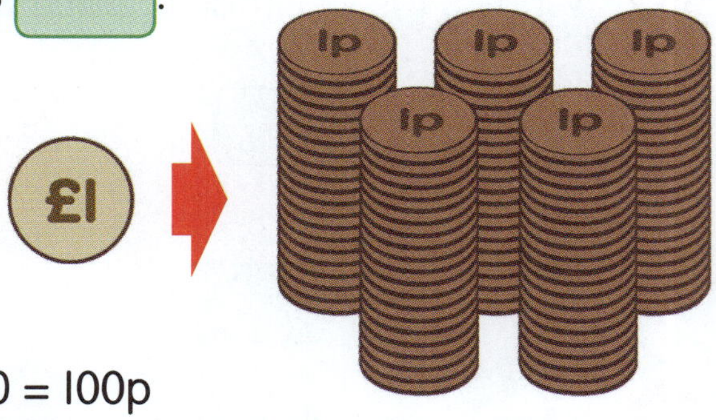

One pound → £1·00 = 100p

a 70p = £0·70 b 17p = £0·17 c 7p = £0·07

25 Change pence to pounds.

a 30p = £ ____ b 53p = £ ____ c 3p = £ ____

26 Write each amount of money as a decimal.

a 5 pounds 20 pence = £5·20 b 7 pounds 45 pence = £ ____

c 18 pounds = £ ____ d 33 pounds 5 pence = £ ____

Practice Book 4B, p.11

Let's Learn!

Understanding thousandths

1

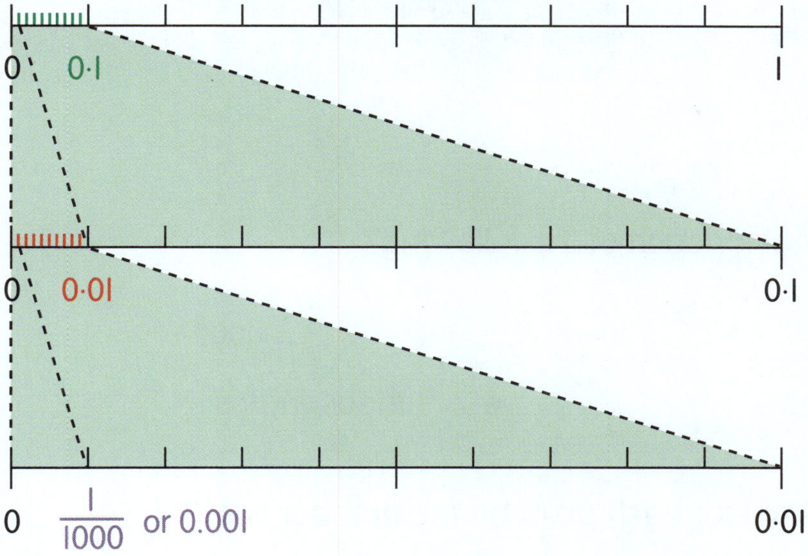

First divide 1 into ten equal parts. Each part is 1 tenth or 0·1.
Then divide 1 tenth into ten equal parts. Each part is 1 hundredth or 0·01.
Finally divide 1 hundredth into ten equal parts.

Each part is $\frac{1}{1000}$ **(one-thousandth)**.

We write $\frac{1}{1000}$ as **0·001** as a decimal.

0·001 = $\frac{1}{1000}$ or 1 thousandth
We read 0·001 as
zero point zero zero one.

2 Here is another way of showing 0·001.
The shaded part is 1 cube out of
1000 cubes.

$\frac{1}{1000}$ = 1 thousandth = 0·001

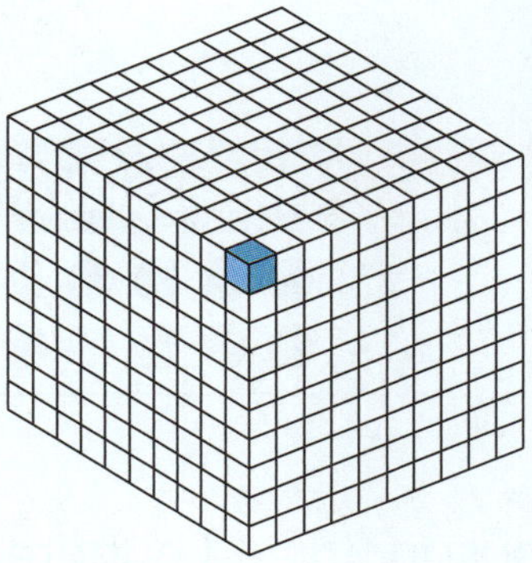

3

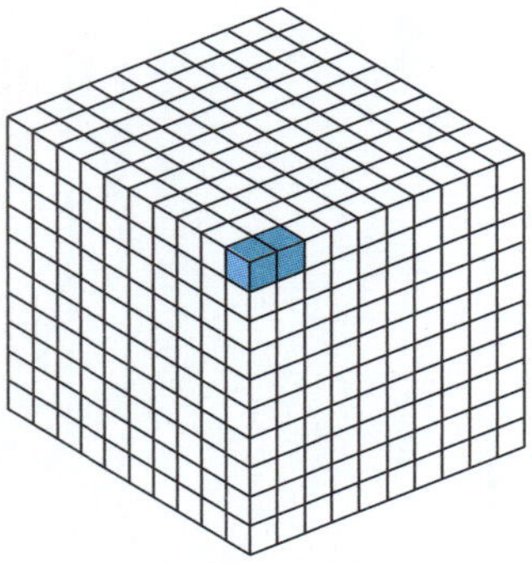

2 thousandths

$\frac{2}{1000}$ = 2 thousandths = 0·002

In the same way $\frac{3}{1000}$ = 0·003

and $\frac{4}{1000}$ = 0·004

4 What is the decimal for each of the following?

a $\frac{5}{1000}$ **b** $\frac{6}{1000}$ **c** $\frac{7}{1000}$

d 8 thousandths **e** 9 thousandths

5 Work out the decimal for each point on the number line.

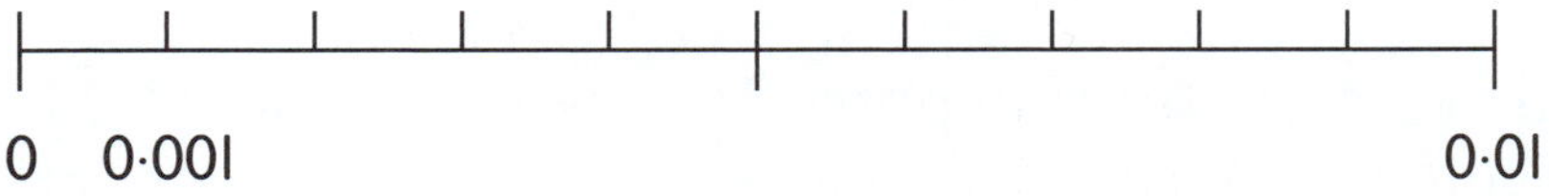

6

10 thousandths

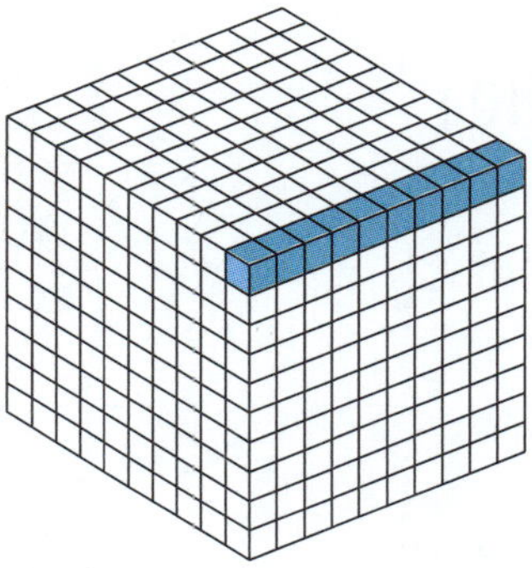

$\frac{10}{1000} = \frac{10 \div 10}{1000 \div 10} = \frac{1}{100}$ or 0·01

10 thousandths = 1 hundredth

You can exchange 10 thousandths for 1 hundredth.

7 Write 3 hundredths 3 thousandths as a decimal.

Ones	Tenths	Hundredths	Thousandths
		● ● ●	● ● ●
0 ·	0	3	3

3 hundredths 3 thousandths = 0·033

We read 0·033 as **zero point zero three three**.

8 What is the decimal for each of the following?

a

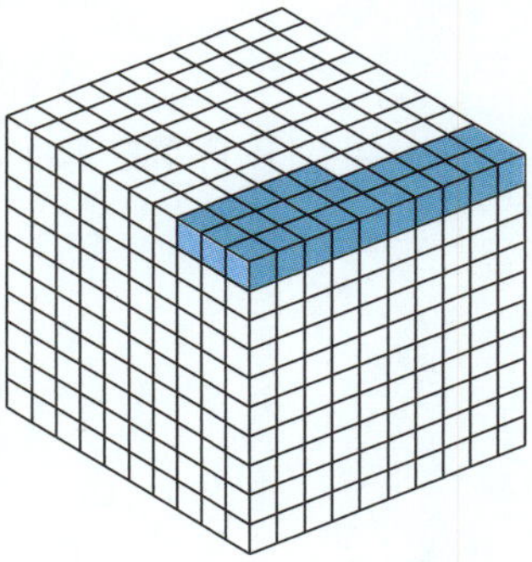

shaded parts = ☐

b

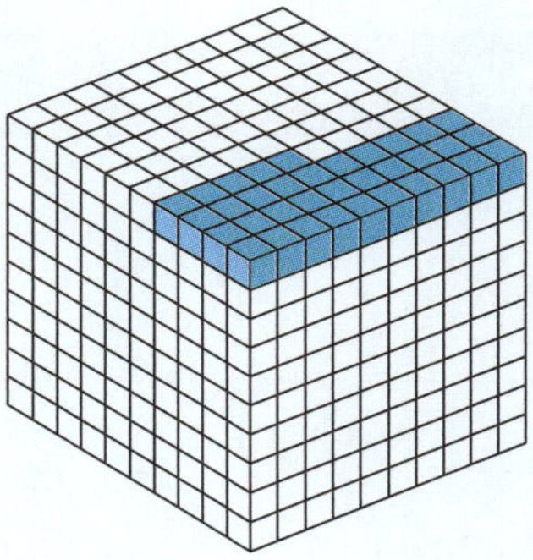

shaded parts = ☐

c

Ones	Tenths	Hundredths	Thousandths
	●	● ● ● ● ● ● ● ● ●	● ● ● ● ● ● ● ● ●

☐

d

Ones	Tenths	Hundredths	Thousandths
			● ● ● ● ● ● ● ● ● ● ● ● ● ●

☐

10 thousandths = **1 hundredth**.

e

Ones	Tenths	Hundredths	Thousandths
●	● ● ●	● ● ● ● ● ● ● ●	● ● ● ● ● ● ● ● ● ● ● ● ●

☐

9 Change $\frac{12}{1000}$ to a decimal.

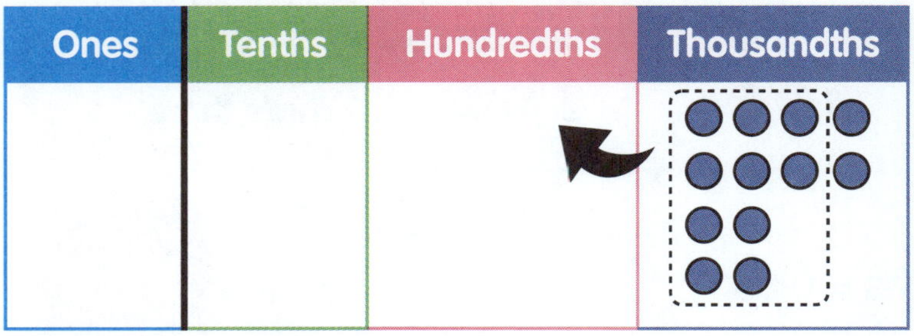

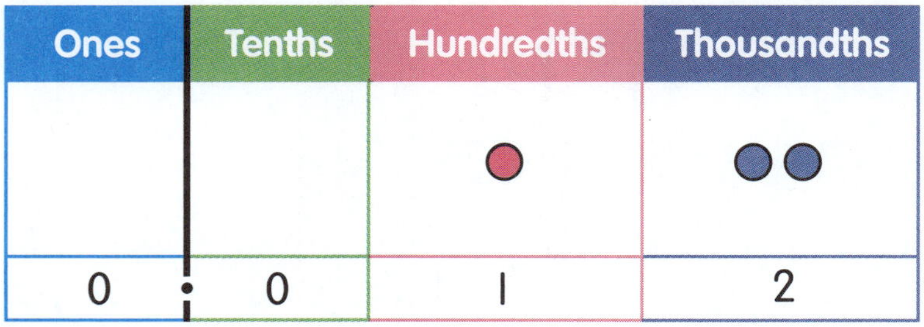

$\frac{12}{1000}$ = 12 thousandths

10 thousandths = 1 hundredth

12 thousandths → 1 hundredth, 2 thousandths

$\frac{12}{1000}$ = 1 hundredth 2 thousandths
= 0·012

10 Change $\frac{112}{1000}$ to a decimal.

$\frac{112}{1000}$ = 1 tenth 12 thousandths
= 1 tenth 1 hundredth 2 thousandths
= 0·112

$\frac{112}{1000}$ = 112 thousandths

100 thousandths = 1 tenth

112 thousandths → 1 tenth, 12 thousandths

11 Change $\frac{2112}{1000}$ to a decimal.

$\frac{2112}{1000}$ = 2 ones 112 thousandths
= 2 ones 1 tenth 1 hundredth
2 thousandths
= 2·112

$\frac{2112}{1000}$ = 2112 thousandths

2000 thousandths = 2 ones

2112 thousandths → 2 ones, 112 thousandths

12 Change $2\frac{372}{1000}$ to a decimal.

Ones	Tenths	Hundredths	Thousandths
●●	●●●	●●●●●●●	●●
2	3	7	2

$2\frac{372}{1000}$ = 2 ones 3 tenths 7 hundredths 2 thousandths

= 2·372

13 What is the decimal for each of the following?

a $\frac{38}{1000}$ g = ___ g

b $\frac{287}{1000}$ ml = ___ ml

c $\frac{1001}{1000}$ km = ___ km

d $2\frac{103}{1000}$ m = ___ m

e $2\frac{4}{1000}$ km = ___ km

f $\frac{4972}{1000}$ m = ___ m

g $4\frac{715}{1000}$ km = ___ km

h $2\frac{4}{1000}$ m = ___ m

14 Does 0·07 have the same value as 0·070? Why?

15

Ones	Tenths	Hundredths	Thousandths
8 •	4	0	9

8·409 = 8 ones 4 tenths 9 thousandths

= 8 + 0·4 + 0·009

$= 8 + \frac{\square}{10} + \frac{\square}{1000}$

16 Find the missing numbers.

a 7·251 = ☐ ones ☐ tenths ☐ hundredths ☐ thousandth

= 7 + 0·2 + 0·05 + ☐

$= 7 + \frac{\square}{10} + \frac{\square}{100} + \frac{\square}{1000}$

b $6{\cdot}656 = 6 + \frac{656}{\square}$

17 In 2·315:

the digit 2 is in the ones place.
the digit 3 stands for 3 tenths or 0·3.
the digit 1 stands for 1 hundredth or 0·01.
the value of the digit 5 is 0·005.

18 Answer these questions.

a In 3·465, the digit 5 is in the ☐ place.

b In 4·732, the digit 7 stands for ☐.

c In 26·019, the value of the digit 1 is ☐.

Game

19

Players: 2

You will need:

- rectangular pieces of paper

1 Write these decimals on rectangular pieces of paper.

0·235 0·471

0·504 0·712

0·673 0·028

0·895 0·808

2 Shuffle the pieces of paper. Player I takes a piece of paper. Player 2 rewrites the decimal on it in at least two different ways.

Example

If the decimal picked was 0·813, it can be rewritten as:

- 8 tenths I hundredth 3 thousandths
- 813 thousandths
- 8 tenths 13 thousandths

3 Player I checks the answers. Take turns to play. Play four rounds each.

The player with the most correct answers wins.

Practice Book 4B, p.15

Let's Learn!

Comparing decimals

1

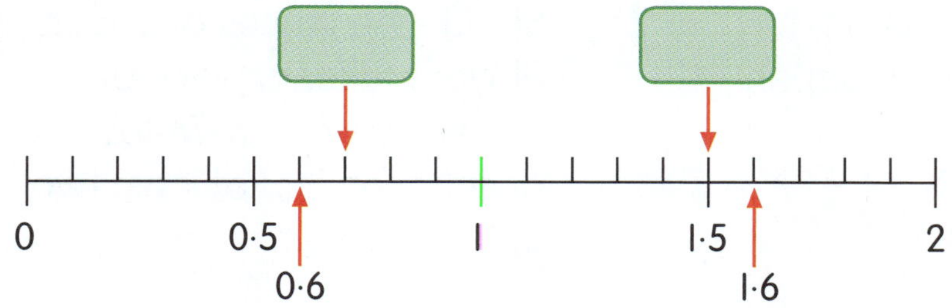

a What is 0·1 more than 0·6?

0·7 is 0·1 more than 0·6.

b What is 0·1 less than 1·6?

1·5 is 0·1 less than 1·6.

2

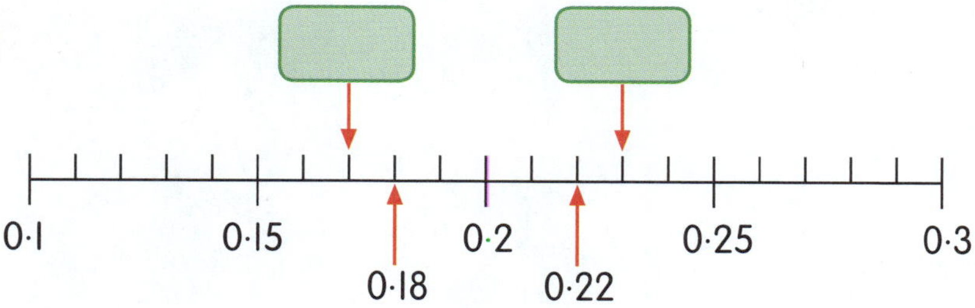

a What is 0·01 more than 0·22?

0·23 is 0·01 more than 0·22.

b What is 0·01 less than 0·18?

0·17 is 0·01 less than 0·18.

3

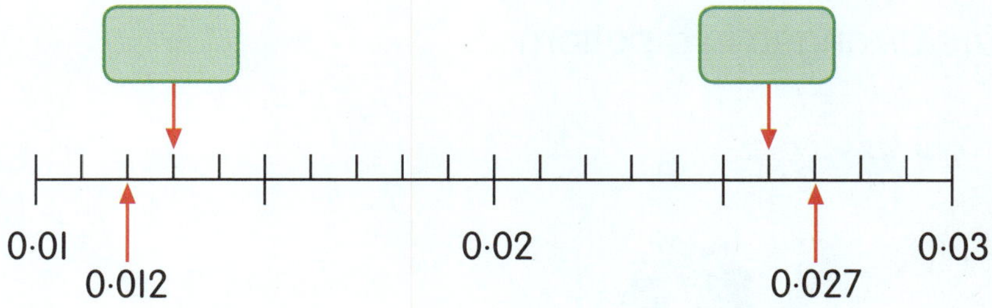

a What is 0·001 more than 0·012?

b What is 0·001 less than 0·027?

4 Answer these questions.

a **i** What number is 0·1 more than 1·2?

ii What number is 0·1 less than 0·9?

iii 0·2 more than 8·7 is ____.

iv 0·5 less than 4·9 is ____.

b **i** What number is 0·01 more than 0·15?

ii What number is 0·01 less than 0·29?

iii 0·02 more than 6·24 is ____.

iv 0·04 less than 7·16 is ____.

c **i** What number is 0·001 more than 0·215?

ii What number is 0·001 less than 0·424?

iii 0·002 more than 4·015 is ____.

iv 0·005 less than 3·147 is ____.

5 These decimals are arranged in a pattern.

0·2, 0·4, 0·6, 0·8, 1·0, ...

+ 0·2 + 0·2 + 0·2

..., 0·4, 0·6, ...

Add 0·2 to get the next number.

What are the next two decimals?

6 These decimals are arranged in a pattern.

1·12, 1·17, 1·22, 1·27, 1·32, ...

+ 0·05 + 0·05 + 0·05

..., 1·17, 1·22, ...

Add 0·05 to get the next number.

What are the next two decimals?

7 These decimals are arranged in a pattern.

1·464, 1·462, 1·460, 1·458, 1·456, ...

− 0·002 − 0·002 − 0·002

..., 1·464, 1·462, ...

Subtract 0·002 to get the next number.

What are the next two decimals?

Practice Book 4B, p.19

8 Which is greater, 0·4 or 0·34?

Ones	Tenths	Hundredths
0 ·	4	
0 ·	3	4

In the same way as comparing whole numbers, we start from the left.

First compare the **ones**. They are the same.
Then compare the **tenths**.
4 tenths is greater than 3 tenths.
So 0·4 is **greater than** 0·34.

9 Arrange 0·62, 0·263 and 0·6 in order. Begin with the smallest.

Ones	Tenths	Hundredths	Thousandths
0 ·	6	2	
0 ·	2	6	3
0 ·	6		

First compare the **ones**.
They are the same.
Then compare the **tenths**.
6 tenths is greater than 2 tenths.
So 0·263 is the smallest.

As 0·62 and 0·6 have the same tenths, compare the **hundredths**.
2 hundredths is greater than 0 hundredths.
So 0·62 is greater than 0·6.
The order beginning with the smallest is 0·263, 0·6, 0·62.

10 Which is greater?

a 0·76 or 0·8

b 0·4 or 0·234

c 0·012 or 0·12

d 0·303 or 0·33

11 Arrange the decimals in order. Begin with the smallest.

a 0·8, 0·17, 0·315

b 0·18, 0·2, 0·185

c 1·004, 0·04, 0·104

d 0·202, 0·022, 0·22

You can use place value charts to help you compare these decimals.

Practice Book 4B, p.23

Game

Players: 2
You will need:
- 12 cards

12 How to play:

1 Make a set of cards using these decimals:

0·5	0·05	0·6	0·07
0·17	1·7	0·71	0·16
1·5	1·06	1·61	0·76

2 Shuffle the cards. Player 1 takes 3 cards. They arrange the decimals in order, beginning with the smallest. Player 2 checks the answer.

3 Return the card to the pack and shuffle it. Take turns to play. Play three rounds each.

The player with the most correct answers wins.

Game

Players: 3

13 How to play:

1 Player 1 thinks of a decimal between 0 and 1. They tell the other players the decimal.

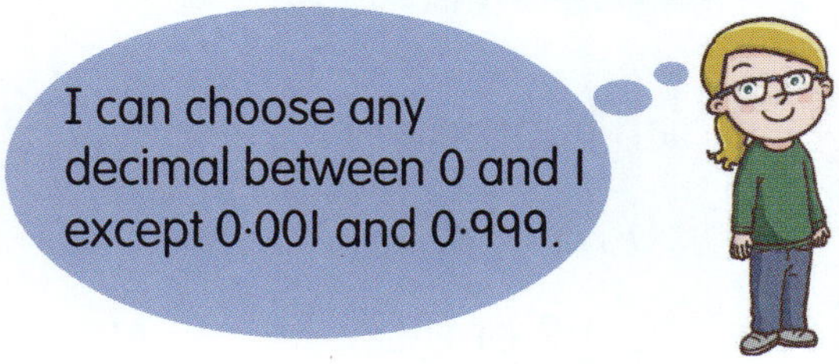

2 Player 2 says a decimal between 0 and 1 that is greater than Player 1's decimal.

3 Player 3 says a decimal between 0 and 1 that is smaller than the first player's decimal.

Take turns to think of a decimal between 0 and 1. Play two rounds each. At each round, the players discuss their answers.

Let's Explore!

14 Your teacher will give you a decimal (for example, 2·58).

1 Insert a zero at any place in this decimal (for example, 2·058).

2 Compare the decimal you made with the original decimal. Then say whether it is greater than, smaller than or equal to the original decimal.

Ones	Tenths	Hundredths	Thousandths
2	5	8	
2	0	5	8

3 Next insert the zero in a different place (for example, 2·580). Then say whether the number is greater than, smaller than or equal to the original decimal.

4 Repeat step 3 until you have inserted a zero in all the different possible places in the original decimal.

Discuss with your friends how inserting a zero into different places in a decimal changes its value.

Let's Learn! 

Rounding decimals

1

The height of a statue is about 8·6 m.
Round 8·6 to the nearest whole number.

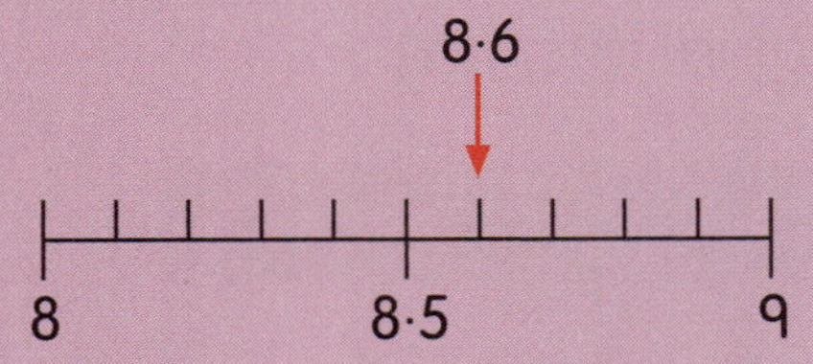

8·6 is between 8 and 9.
It is nearer to 9 than to 8.
8·6 is 9 when rounded to the nearest whole number.
So 8·6 ≈ 9.

2

The mass of these potatoes is 35·2 kg. What is their mass to the nearest kilogram?

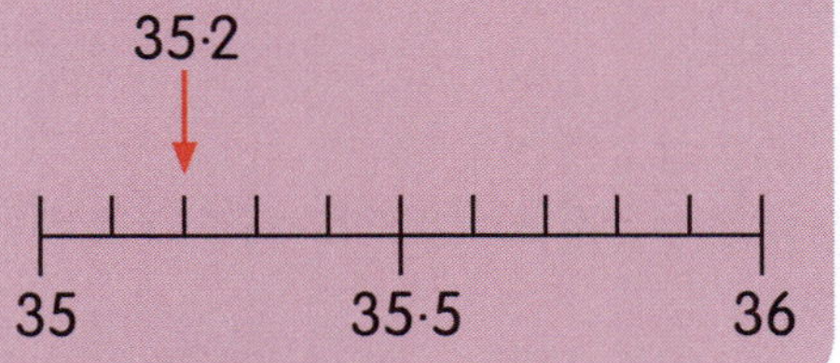

35·2 is between 35 and 36. It is nearer to 35 than to 36.
35·2 is 35 when rounded to the nearest whole number.
So 35·2 ≈ 35.
The mass of potatoes to the nearest kilogram is 35 kg.

3 Round 26·5 to the nearest whole number.

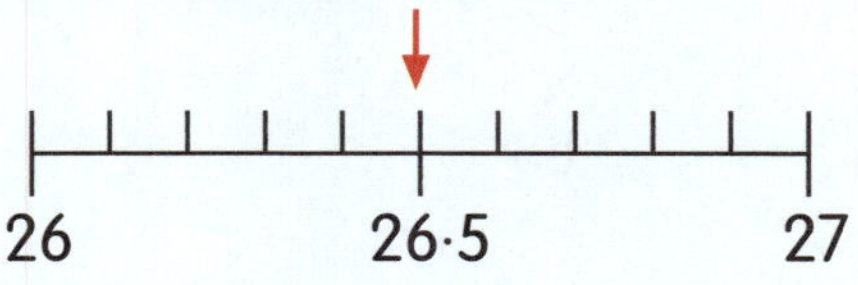

26·5 is exactly halfway between 26 and 27.
We round it to 27.
26·5 is 27 when rounded to the nearest whole number.
So 26·5 ≈ 27.

4 Round 14·68 to the nearest whole number.

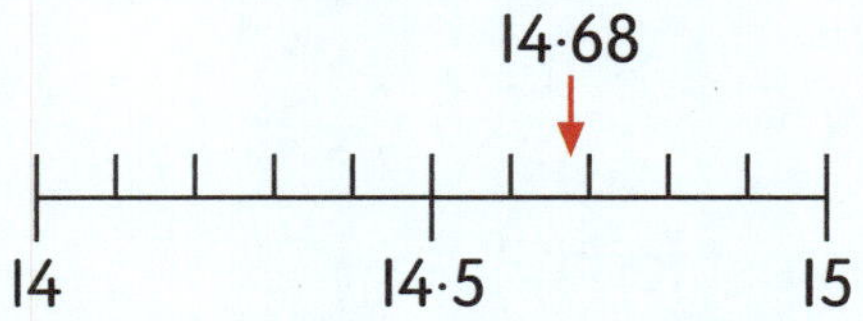

14·68 is between 14 and 15. It is nearer to 15 than to 14.
14·68 is 15 when rounded to the nearest whole number.
So 14·68 ≈ 15.

5 Round 39·45 to the nearest whole number.

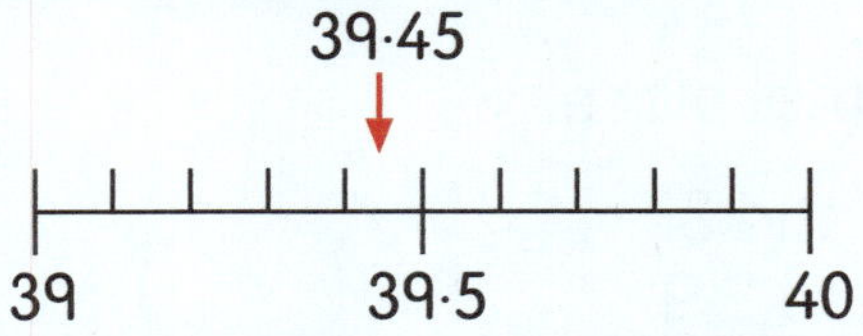

39·45 is between 39 and 40. It is nearer to 39 than to 40.
39·45 is 39 when rounded to the nearest whole number.
So 39·45 ≈ 39.

6 For each decimal, draw a number line. Use a cross (X) to show where the decimal is on the number line. Then round it to the nearest whole number.

Example

5.8

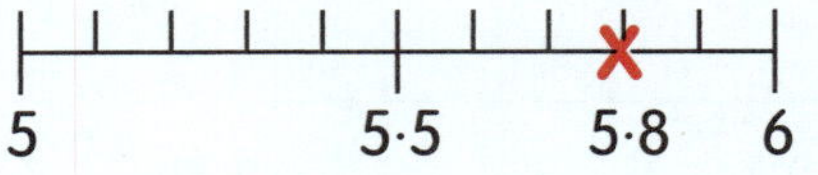

5·8 is 6 when rounded to the nearest whole number.

a 0·45 **b** 0·7 **c** 4·3 **d** 12·5

Practice Book 4B, p.25

7 Liam's height is 0·83 m. Round 0·83 to the nearest tenth or 1 decimal place.

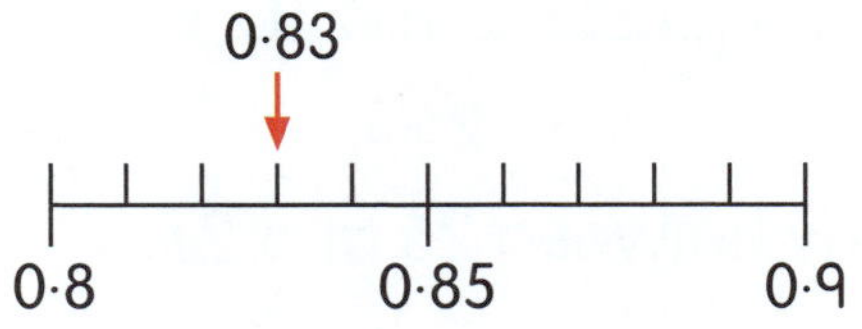

0·83 = 8 tenths 3 hundredths
0·83 is between 8 tenths (0·8) and 9 tenths (0·9).
It is nearer to 0·8 than to 0·9.
0·83 is 0·8 when rounded to the nearest tenth or 1 decimal place.
So 0·83 ≈ 0·8.

8 Round 1·75 to the nearest tenth.

1·75 is exactly halfway between 1·7 and 1·8.
We round it to 1·8.
1·75 is 1·8 when rounded to the nearest tenth.
So 1·75 ≈ 1·8.

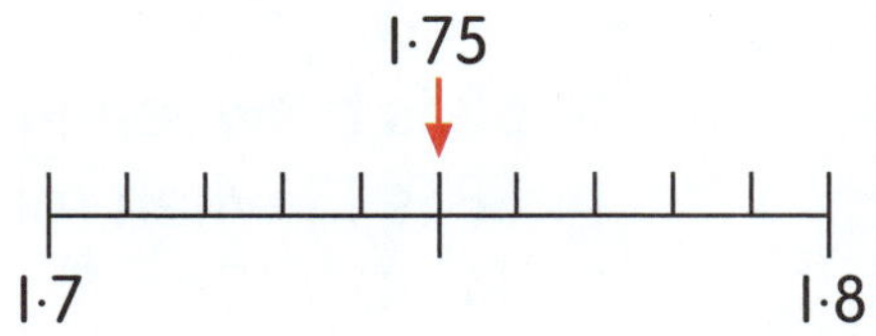

9 Round 2·98 to 1 decimal place.

2·98 is between 2·9 and 3.
It is nearer to 3 than to 2·9.
2·98 is 3·0 when rounded to 1 decimal place.
So 2·98 ≈ 3·0.

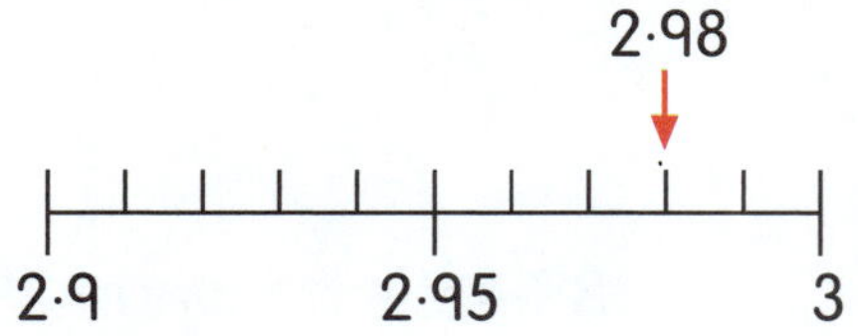

3 is written as 3·0 to 1 decimal place.

10 For each decimal, draw a number line. Use a cross (X) to show where the decimal is on the number line. Then round it to 1 decimal place.

Example

3·43

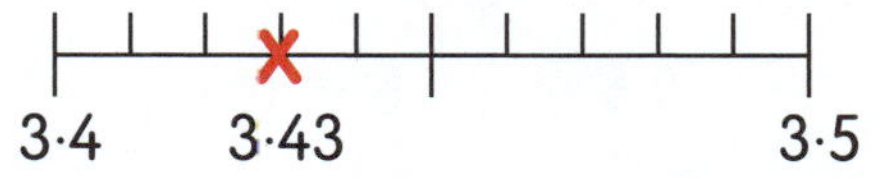

3·43 is 3·4 when rounded to 1 decimal place.

a 0·36 **b** 4·32 **c** 4·05

11 A sheet of plastic is 0·014 cm thick. Round 0·014 to the nearest hundredth or 2 decimal places.

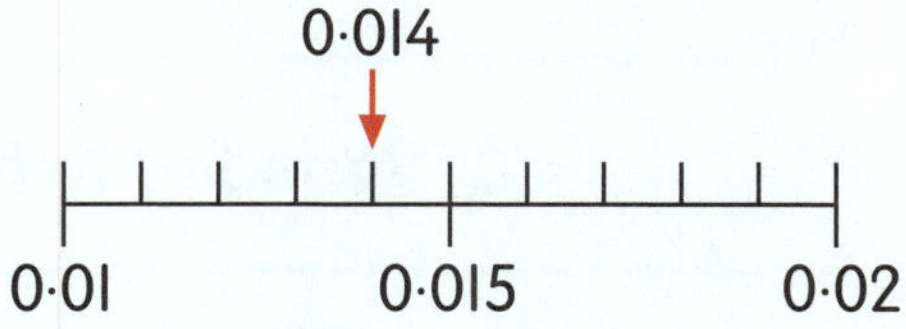

0·014 = 1 hundredth 4 thousandths
0·014 is between 1 hundredth (0·01) and 2 hundredths (0·02).
It is nearer to 0·01 than to 0·02.
0·014 is 0·01 when rounded to the nearest hundredth or 2 decimal places.
So 0·014 ≈ 0·01.

12 Round 2·345 to the nearest hundredth.

2·345 is exactly halfway between 2·34 and 2·35.
We round it to 2·35.
2·345 is 2·35 when rounded to the nearest hundredth.
So 2·345 ≈ 2·35.

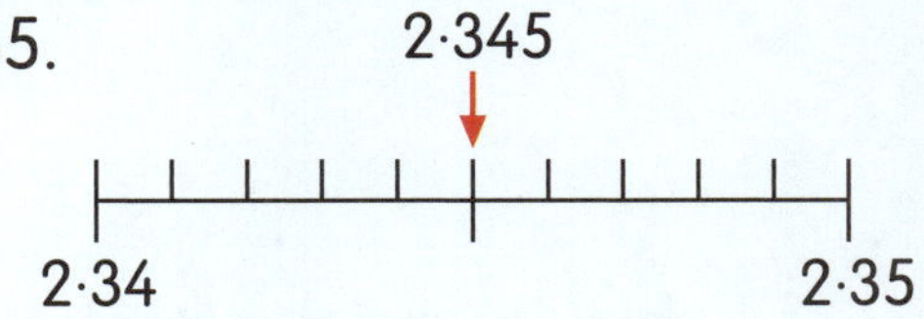

13 Round 5·997 to 2 decimal places.

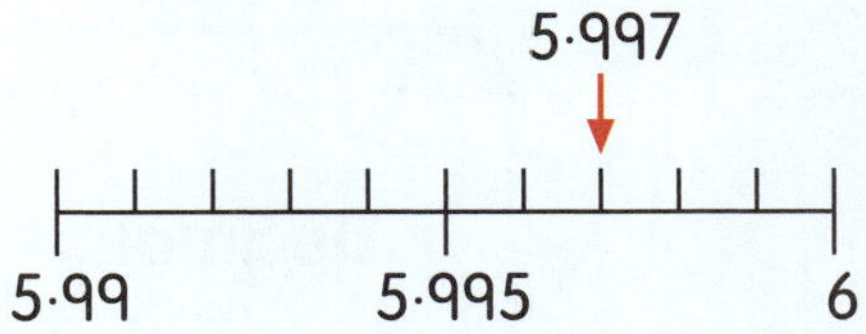

5·997 is between 5·99 and 6.
It is nearer to 6 than to 5·99.
5·997 is 6·00 when rounded to 2 decimal places.
So 5·997 ≈ 6·00.

6 is written as 6·00 to 2 decimal places.

14 For each decimal, draw a number line. Use a cross (X) to show where the decimal is on the number line. Then round it to 2 decimal places.

Example

0·123

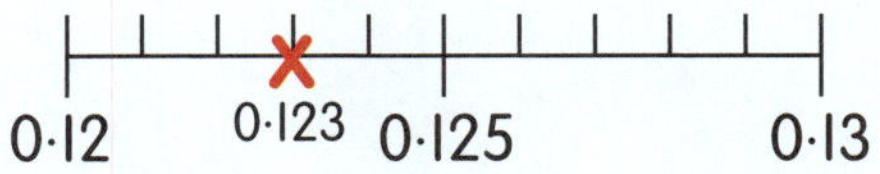

0·123 is 0·12 when rounded to 2 decimal places.

a 0·516 **b** 3·294 **c** 8·995

15 **a** Round the following decimals to the nearest whole number, nearest tenth and nearest hundredth.

Decimal	Rounded to the Nearest		
	Whole Number	Tenth	Hundredth
2·029			
5·783			

b Round the following decimals to the nearest whole number, 1 decimal place and 2 decimal places.

Decimal	Rounded to		
	The Nearest Whole Number	1 Decimal Place	2 Decimal Places
12·705			
25·957			

Practice Book 4B, p.27

Activity

16 Work in pairs.
You have £25·00. You want to buy these items at a supermarket.
Round the cost of each item to 1 decimal place.
Then add to find out whether you have enough money to pay for the items.

Let's Explore!

17 **Example**

A number has 2 decimal places. It is 1·7 when rounded to 1 decimal place. What could the number be?

Tai draws a number line to find the number.

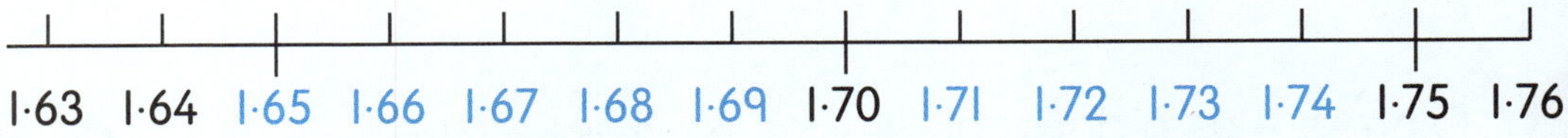

The numbers in blue are the possible answers.

A number has 3 decimal places. It is 2·34 when rounded to 2 decimal places.

a What could the number be? List the possible answers.

b Which of these numbers is the greatest?

c Which of these numbers is the smallest?

Let's Learn!

Fractions and decimals

1 Express the fraction $\frac{1}{5}$ as a decimal.

$$\frac{1}{5} \xrightarrow{\times 2} \frac{2}{10} = 0{\cdot}2$$

(Numerator × 2, denominator × 2)

So $\frac{1}{5}$ is 0·2 as a decimal.

2 Here is another way to show $\frac{1}{5} = 0{\cdot}2$.

Look at the fraction bar and the number line.

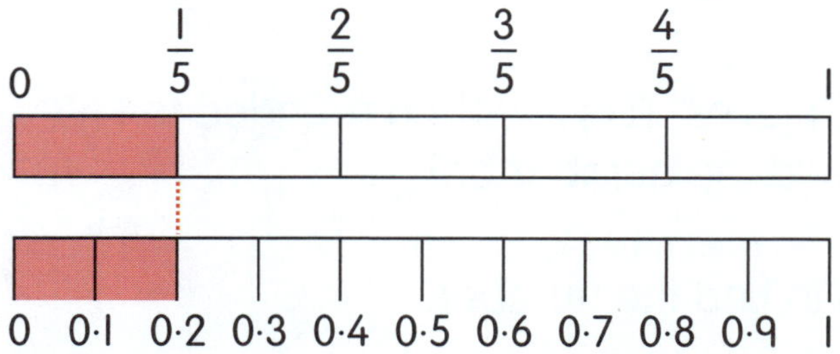

3 Express $\frac{1}{4}$ as a decimal.

$$\frac{1}{4} = \frac{25}{100} = 0{\cdot}25$$

(Numerator × 25, denominator × 25)

So $\frac{1}{4}$ is 0·25 as a decimal.

4 You can see that $\frac{1}{4} = 0{\cdot}25$.

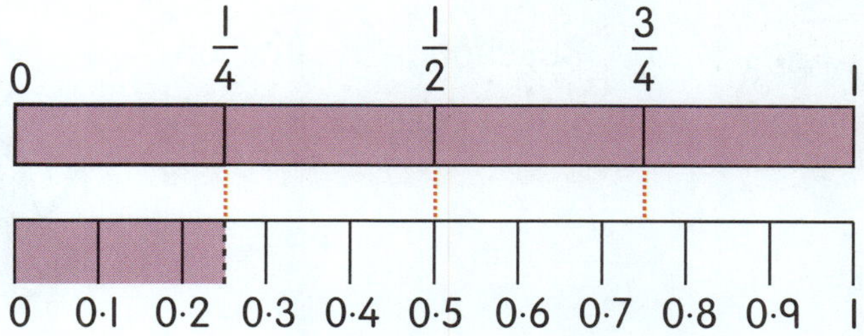

You can also see that $\frac{1}{2} =$ ___ and $\frac{3}{4} =$ ___.

5 Express $\frac{5}{4}$ as a decimal.

$\frac{5}{4} = \frac{4}{4} + \frac{1}{4}$

$= 1 + \frac{1}{4}$

$= 1 + 0{\cdot}25$

$= 1{\cdot}25$

6 Express $\frac{8}{5}$ as a decimal.

$\frac{8}{5} = \frac{5}{5} + \frac{\text{\_\_\_}}{5}$

$= 1 +$ ___

$=$ ___

7 Express each fraction as a decimal.

a $\frac{3}{5}$　**b** $\frac{5}{2}$　**c** $\frac{9}{20}$

d $\frac{3}{2}$　**e** $\frac{7}{5}$　**f** $\frac{11}{4}$

8 Express $3\frac{1}{2}$ as a decimal.

$$\frac{1}{2} = \frac{1 \times 5}{2 \times 5} = \frac{5}{10} = 0{\cdot}5$$

$$3\frac{1}{2} = \frac{7}{2} = \frac{7 \times 5}{2 \times 5} = \frac{35}{10} = 3{\cdot}5$$

$3\frac{1}{2}$ is 3·5 as a decimal.

9 Express each mixed number as a decimal.

a $2\frac{3}{5}$ **b** $9\frac{1}{4}$ **c** $1\frac{8}{20}$ **d** $5\frac{27}{50}$

10 Express 0·8 as a fraction in its simplest form.

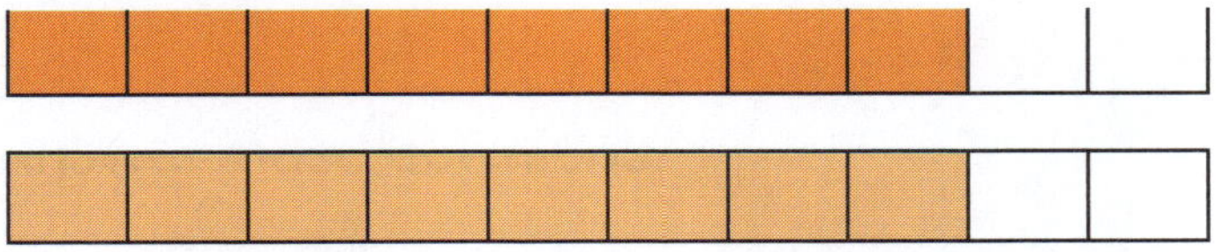

$$0{\cdot}8 = \frac{8}{10} = \frac{4}{5}$$

11 Express 2·5 as a mixed number in its simplest form.

$$2{\cdot}5 = \frac{25}{10}$$
$$= \frac{20}{10} + \frac{5}{10}$$
$$= 2 + \frac{5}{10}$$
$$= 2 + \frac{1}{2}$$
$$= 2\frac{1}{2}$$

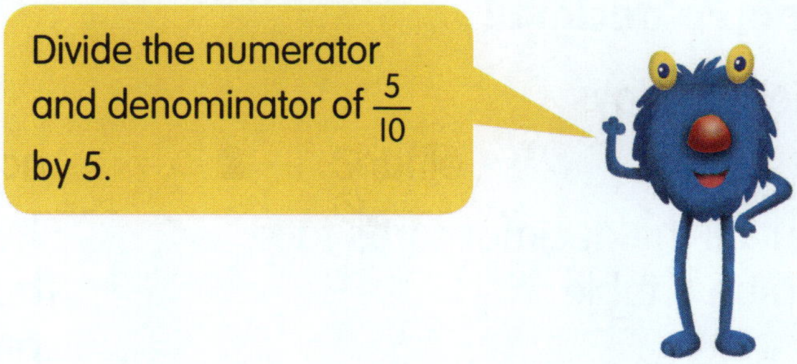

12 Express 7·25 as a mixed number in its simplest form.

$$7{\cdot}25 = 7 + 0{\cdot}25$$
$$= 7 + \frac{25}{100}$$
$$= 7 + \frac{1}{4}$$
$$= 7\frac{1}{4}$$

13 Express each decimal as a fraction or a mixed number in its simplest form.

a 0·4 **b** 2·8 **c** 3·75

d 0·6 **e** 5·2 **f** 2·45

g 2·75 **h** 4·35 **i** 8·72

Practice Book 4B, p.31

Game

Players: 4 or 5

You will need:

- decimal cards
- fraction cards

14 Snap a decimal!

How to play:

1 Put all the decimal cards face up on a table.

2 Shuffle the fraction cards. Then turn over the fraction card at the top of the pack.

3 Check if the fraction on the card shown is equivalent to any of the decimals on the table.

For example, the fraction $\frac{1}{5}$ is equivalent to the decimal 0·2.

4 The fastest player to find a match calls out "decimal snap", and collects the two cards.

The other players check the answer. If the answer is wrong, the cards are taken away from the player and put back on the table and at the bottom of the fraction cards pack.

5 Turn over the next fraction card to continue the game. Play until no more matches can be found.

The player who collects the most matching cards wins.

Maths Journal

15 Peter and Miya think that 0·23 is greater than 0·3.

Explain to your friends why Peter and Miya are wrong.

Put On Your Thinking Caps!

16 You will need a strip of paper of this length and size.

Its length is 1 unit. Estimate in **tenths** the length of these lines using the paper strip.

Example

estimated length = 0·7 units

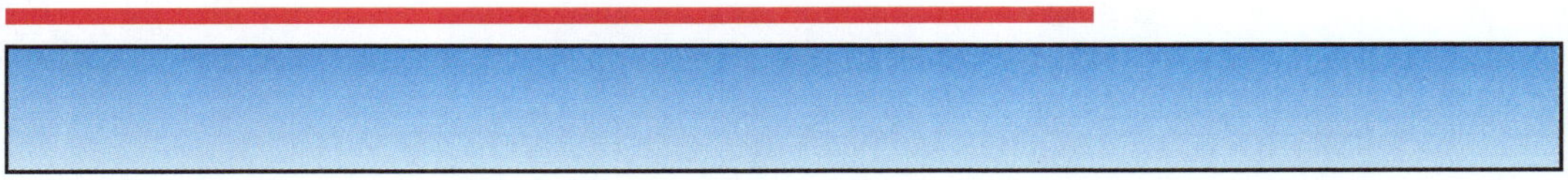

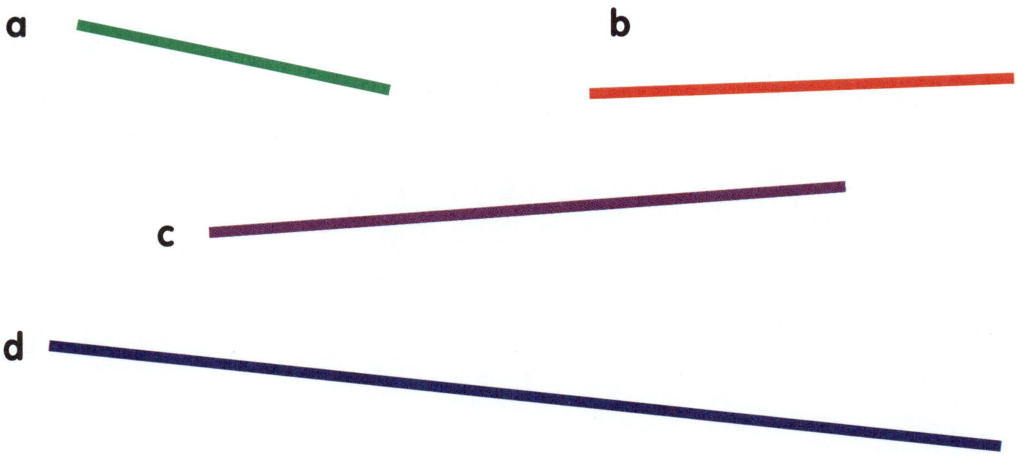

How can you check whether your estimate is accurate?

Put On Your Thinking Caps!

17 You will need a strip of paper with markings as shown.

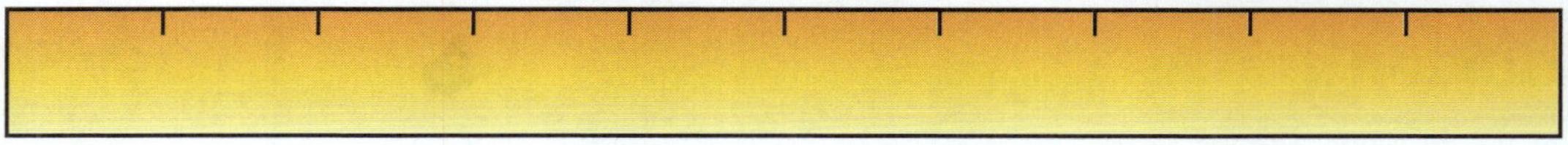

Its length is 1 unit. Estimate in **hundredths** the length of these lines using the paper strip.

Example

estimated length = 0·65 units

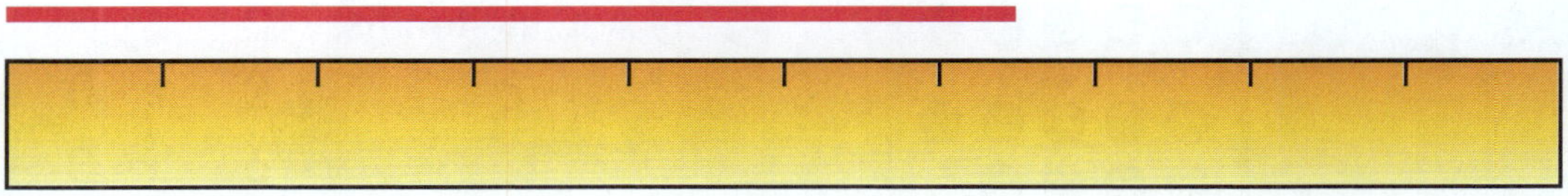

Practice Book 4B, p.33
Practice Book 4B, p.34

Unit 10 Decimals (2)

Let's Learn!

Addition

1 Ella hopped 0·4 m from the starting line.
Ruby hopped a distance of 0·5 m.
How far did they hop altogether?

0·4 + 0·5 = ?

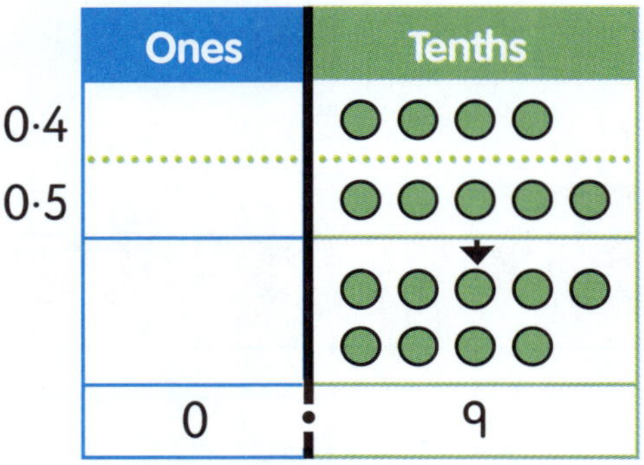

So 0·4 + 0·5 = 0·9.

They hopped 0·9 m altogether.

Write the numbers with the decimal points aligned.

Add the **tenths**.

```
    0 · 4
+   0 · 5
---------
    0 · 9
```

4 tenths + 5 tenths = 9 tenths

2 Add 0·6 and 0·7.

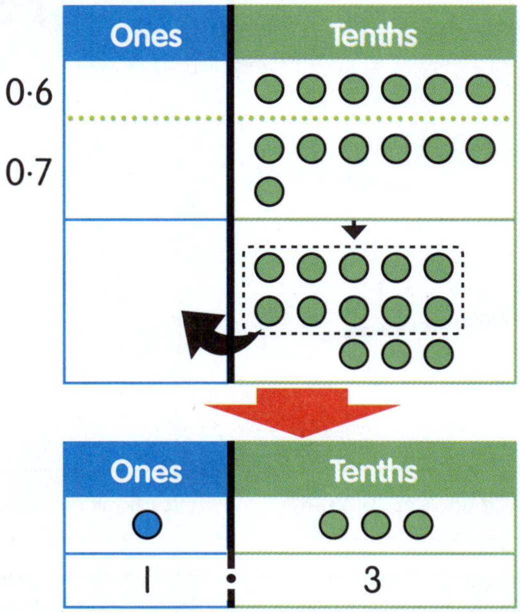

So 0·6 + 0·7 = 1·3.

Write the numbers with the decimal points aligned.

Add the **tenths**.

```
    0 · 6
+   0 · 7
---------
    1 · 3
    1
```

6 tenths + 7 tenths
= 13 tenths
= 1 one 3 tenths

3 Find the value of 5·4 + 7·8.

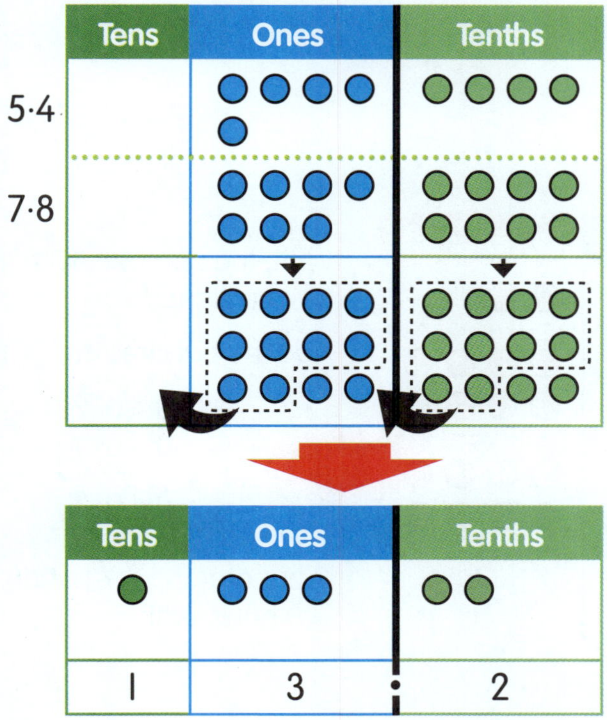

So 5·4 + 7·8 = ____.

Write the numbers with the decimal points aligned.

First add the **tenths**.

```
   5 · 4
+  7 · 8
--------
     · 2
--------
   1
```

4 tenths + 8 tenths

= ____ tenths

= ____ one ____ tenths

Then add the **ones**.

```
   5 · 4
+  7 · 8
--------
 1 3 · 2
--------
   1
```

5 ones + 7 ones + 1 one

= ____ ones

4 Regroup.

a 16 tenths = ____ one ____ tenths

b 3 tenths + 9 tenths = ____ tenths

= ____ one ____ tenths

5 Add.

a

```
   0 · 4
+  0 · 2
--------
   ____
--------
```

b

```
   0 · 5
+  0 · 6
--------
   ____
--------
```

c

```
   3 · 5
+  2 · 9
--------
   ____
--------
```

6 Write in vertical form. Then add.

a 2·3 + 3·9 **b** 5·9 + 8 **c** 7·6 + 4·8

Practice Book 4B, p.35

7 Miya has two 1p coins. Omar has seven 1p coins. How much money do they have altogether?

Two 1p coins is £0·02.
Seven 1p coins is £0·07.
£0·02 + £0·07 = ?

0·02

0·07

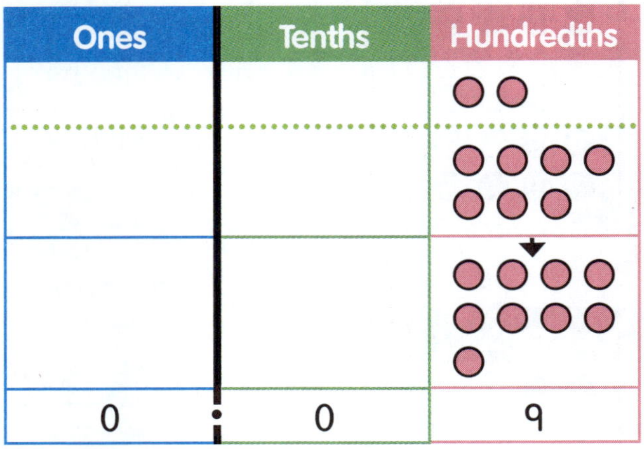

Write the numbers with the decimal points aligned.

Add the **hundredths**.

```
   0 · 0 2
+  0 · 0 7
----------
   0 · 0 9
```

2 hundredths + 7 hundredths
= 9 hundredths

So £0·02 + £0·07 = £ ______ .

They have £ ______ altogether.

8 Add 0·08 and 0·26.

0·08

0·26

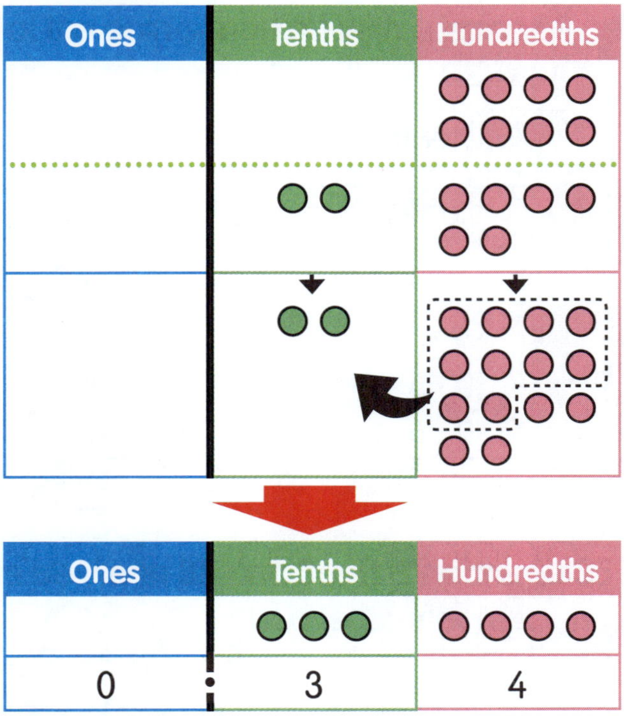

Write the numbers with the decimal points aligned.

First add the **hundredths**.

```
   0 · 0 8
+  0 · 2 6
----------
         4
       1
```

8 hundredths + 6 hundredths
= 14 hundredths
= 1 tenth 4 hundredths

Then add the **tenths**.

```
   0 · 0 8
+  0 · 2 6
----------
   0 · 3 4
       1
```

0 tenths + 2 tenths + 1 tenths
= 3 tenths

So 0·08 + 0·26 = 0·34.

9 Add 1·47 and 3·95.

First add the hundredths.	Then add the tenths.	Finally add the ones.
1·47 + 3·95 = ...2	1·47 + 3·95 = ...42	1·47 + 3·95 = 5·42
7 hundredths + 5 hundredths = 12 hundredths = 1 tenth 2 hundredths	4 tenths + 9 tenths + 1 tenth = 14 tenths = 1 one 4 tenths	1 one + 3 ones + 1 one = 5 ones

So 1·47 + 3·95 = 5·42.

10 Regroup.

a 13 hundredths = ☐ tenth ☐ hundredths

b 7 hundredths + 4 hundredths = ☐ hundredths
= ☐ tenth ☐ hundredth

11 Add.

a 0·08 + 0·04 = ☐

b 0·18 + 0·39 = ☐

c 3·46 + 0·76 = ☐

12 Write in vertical form. Then add.

a 4·5 + 6·48 **b** £10·25 + £6·35 **c** £1·99 + £1·05

Home Maths

Encourage your child to add tenths or hundredths mentally. For example, to add 0·3 and 0·4, ask them to add 3 tenths and 4 tenths mentally to get 7 tenths or 0·7. They can also use mental calculation for subtraction.

Practice Book 4B, p.37

Let's Learn!

Subtraction

1 A bottle contains 0·5 ℓ of water. Peter drinks 0·3 ℓ of water from it. How much water is left in the bottle?

0·5 – 0·3 = ?

Ones	Tenths
	○ ○ ⊘ ⊘ ⊘

Write the numbers with the decimal points aligned.

Subtract the **tenths**.

$$\begin{array}{rr} & 0\cdot5 \\ - & 0\cdot3 \\ \hline & 0\cdot2 \\ \hline \end{array}$$

5 tenths – 3 tenths = 2 tenths

So 0·5 – 0·3 = 0·2.

0·2 ℓ of water is left in the bottle.

2 Subtract.

a $\begin{array}{rr} & 0\cdot9 \\ - & 0\cdot1 \\ \hline & \square \\ \hline \end{array}$

b $\begin{array}{rr} & 3\cdot5 \\ - & 1\cdot4 \\ \hline & \square \\ \hline \end{array}$

c $\begin{array}{rr} & 9\cdot9 \\ - & 0\cdot9 \\ \hline & \square \\ \hline \end{array}$

d $\begin{array}{rr} & 0\cdot8 \\ - & 0\cdot5 \\ \hline & \square \\ \hline \end{array}$

e $\begin{array}{rr} & 0\cdot9 \\ - & 0\cdot3 \\ \hline & \square \\ \hline \end{array}$

f $\begin{array}{rr} & 5\cdot8 \\ - & 2\cdot1 \\ \hline & \square \\ \hline \end{array}$

3 Write in vertical form. Then subtract.

a 8·9 – 7·8 **b** 7·3 – 4

c 10·7 – 2·1 **d** 8·4 – 2·4

Remember to align the decimal points when you write in the vertical form.

4 Subtract 0·7 from 1·5.

1·5

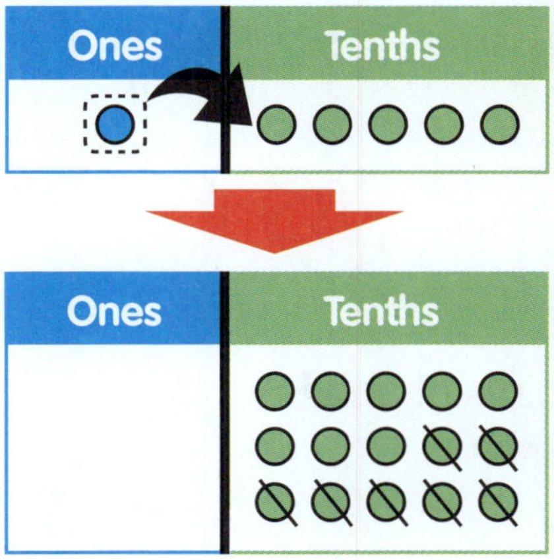

We can't subtract 7 tenths from 5 tenths. Regroup 1 one 5 tenths.

1 one 5 tenths = 15 tenths

Write the numbers with the decimal points aligned.

Subtract the **tenths**.

$$\begin{array}{rcl} \overset{0}{\not 1} & \cdot & {}^{1}5 \\ -\ 0 & \cdot & 7 \\ \hline 0 & \cdot & 8 \\ \hline \end{array}$$

15 tenths – 7 tenths = 8 tenths

Regroup: 1 one 5 tenths = 15 tenths

Take away 7 tenths.

So 1·5 – 0·7 = 0·8.

5 Regroup.

a 1 = ☐ tenths **b** 2·5 = ☐ tenths

c 6 = 5 ones ☐ tenths **d** 1·6 = ☐ tenths

e 8·7 = 7 ones ☐ tenths **f** 2·4 = 1 one ☐ tenths

6 Subtract.

a
$$\begin{array}{r} 1\cdot 0 \\ -\ 0\cdot 4 \\ \hline \square \\ \hline \end{array}$$

b
$$\begin{array}{r} 7\cdot 2 \\ -\ 0\cdot 5 \\ \hline \square \\ \hline \end{array}$$

c
$$\begin{array}{r} 1\cdot 5 \\ -\ 0\cdot 8 \\ \hline \square \\ \hline \end{array}$$

7 Write in vertical form. Then subtract.

a 3·5 – 2·7 **b** 5·8 – 3·9 **c** 8·1 – 2·4

8 Subtract 0·8 from 2.

We can write 2 as 2·0.
Write the numbers with the decimal points aligned.
We cannot subtract 8 tenths from 0 tenths.

Regroup 2 ones.

$$\begin{array}{r} {}^{1}\not{2}\cdot{}^{1}0 \\ -\ 0\cdot 8 \\ \hline \\ \hline \end{array}$$

2 ones = 1 one 10 tenths

First subtract the **tenths**.

$$\begin{array}{r} {}^{1}\not{2}\cdot{}^{1}0 \\ -\ 0\cdot 8 \\ \hline \cdot 2 \\ \hline \end{array}$$

Then subtract the **ones**.

$$\begin{array}{r} {}^{1}\not{2}\cdot{}^{1}0 \\ -\ 0\cdot 8 \\ \hline 1\cdot 2 \\ \hline \end{array}$$

2·0 – 0·8 = 1·2

9 Write in vertical form. Then subtract.

a 6 – 3·6 **b** 10 – 7·4

c 8 – 2·5 **d** 11 – 3·2

10 Find the value of 3·24 – 1·06.

We can't subtract 6 hundredths from 4 hundredths.
Regroup 3 ones 2 tenths 4 hundredths.

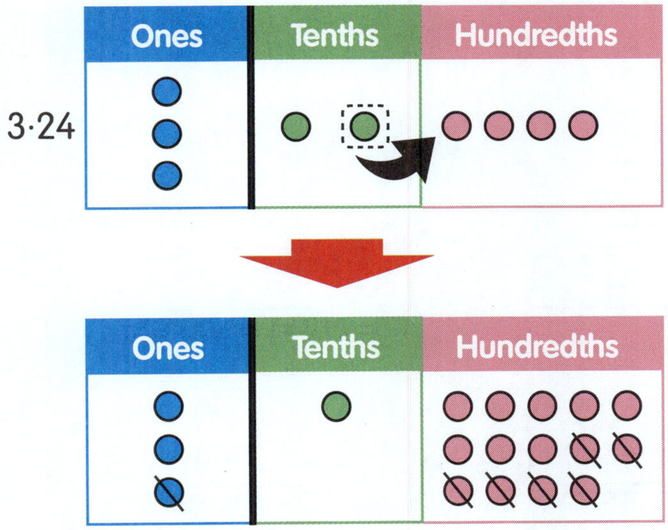

3 ones 2 tenths 4 hundredths
= 3 ones 1 tenth 14 hundredths
Write the numbers with the decimal points aligned.

First subtract the **hundredths**.

$$\begin{array}{rcccc} & 3 & \cdot & \overset{1}{\not{2}} & {}^{1}4 \\ - & 1 & \cdot & 0 & 6 \\ \hline & & & & 8 \end{array}$$

14 hundredths – 6 hundredths
= 8 hundredths

Then subtract the **tenths**.

$$\begin{array}{rcccc} & 3 & \cdot & \overset{1}{\not{2}} & {}^{1}4 \\ - & 1 & \cdot & 0 & 6 \\ \hline & & \cdot & 1 & 8 \end{array}$$

1 tenth – 0 tenths = 1 tenth

Finally subtract the **ones**.

$$\begin{array}{rcccc} & 3 & \cdot & \overset{1}{\not{2}} & {}^{1}4 \\ - & 1 & \cdot & 0 & 6 \\ \hline & 2 & \cdot & 1 & 8 \end{array}$$

3 ones – 1 one = 2 ones

So 3·24 – 1·06 = 2·18.

11 Regroup.

a 0·35 = 2 tenths ☐ hundredths

b 1·26 = ☐ one 1 tenth ☐ hundredths

c 8 tenths 2 hundredths = 7 tenths ☐ hundredths

d 5 tenths = 4 tenths ☐ hundredths

e 7 ones 5 tenths = 6 ones ☐ tenths

12 Subtract.

a 0·11 − 0·07 = ☐

b 0·36 − 0·18 = ☐

c 2·35 − 1·19 = ☐

d 0·42 − 0·07 = ☐

e 6·20 − 4·18 = ☐

f 3·90 − 3·89 = ☐

g 2·43 − 1·65 = ☐

h 5·30 − 1·86 = ☐

i 7·10 − 2·06 = ☐

13 Write in vertical form. Then subtract.

a 3·85 – 1·69

b 16·78 – 5·9

c 24·67 – 0·79

d 9·40 – 3·87

14 Subtract 0·38 from 5·5.

We can write 5·5 as 5·50.
Write the numbers with the decimal points aligned.
We cannot subtract 8 hundredths from 0 hundredths.

Regroup 5 tenths.

$$\begin{array}{r} 5\cdot\overset{4}{\cancel{5}}\,{}^{1}0 \\ -\ 0\cdot 3\ 8 \\ \hline \\ \hline \end{array}$$

5 tenths =
4 tenths 10 hundredths

First subtract the **hundredths**.

$$\begin{array}{r} 5\cdot\overset{4}{\cancel{5}}\,{}^{1}0 \\ -\ 0\cdot 3\ 8 \\ \hline 2 \\ \hline \end{array}$$

Then subtract the **tenths**.

$$\begin{array}{r} 5\cdot\overset{4}{\cancel{5}}\,{}^{1}0 \\ -\ 0\cdot 3\ 8 \\ \hline \cdot\ 1\ 2 \\ \hline \end{array}$$

Finally subtract the **ones**.

$$\begin{array}{r} 5\cdot\overset{4}{\cancel{5}}\,{}^{1}0 \\ -\ 0\cdot 3\ 8 \\ \hline 5\cdot 1\ 2 \\ \hline \end{array}$$

5·5 – 0·38 = 5·12

15 Write in vertical form. Then subtract.

a 7·5 – 3·68

b 2 – 0·55

Practice Book 4B, p.41

Let's Learn!

Word problems

1 Farha had £8·50. She spent £3·75 on a book. How much money did she have left?

£8·50 – £3·75 = £4·75

She had £4·75 left.

```
   7  14 10
 £ 8 · 5  0
– £ 3 · 7  5
 ----------
 £ 4 · 7  5
```

2 For a party, Hardeep prepared 2·75 ℓ of lemon squash and 1·26 ℓ of orange squash. How much squash did he prepare altogether?

☐ + ☐ = ☐

He prepared ☐ ℓ of squash altogether.

```
   2 · 7 5
+  1 · 2 6
 ---------
       ☐
```

3 Tom is 0·08 m taller than Amit. Ethan is 0·16 m shorter than Tom. If Ethan is 1·65 m tall, what is Amit's height?

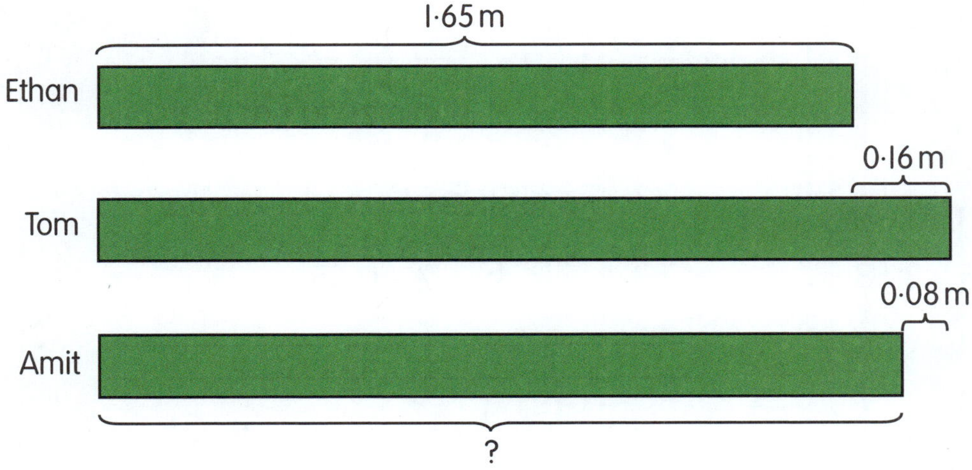

1·65 m + 0·16 m = 1·81 m

Tom's height is 1·81 m.

1·81 m – 0·08 m = 1·73 m

Amit's height is 1·73 m.

4 A coat costs £66·45. A jumper costs £28·65. Ruby's dad has £75.
How much more money does he need to buy the coat and the jumper?

£ ______ + £ ______ = £ ______

The total cost of the coat and the jumper is £ ______.

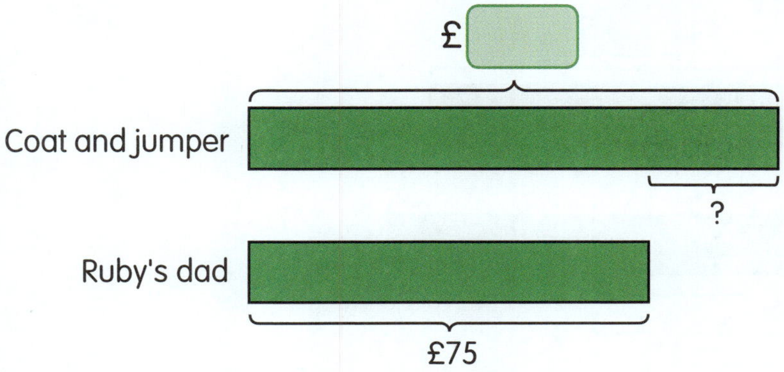

£ ______ − £ ______ = £ ______

He needs £ ______ more to buy the coat and the jumper.

5 A piece of material 4 m long is cut into two pieces. The first piece is 1·25 m long. How much longer is the second piece of material?

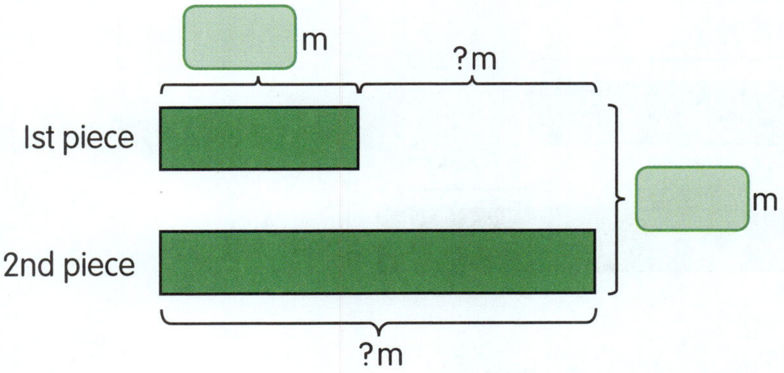

______ m − ______ m = ______ m

The length of the second piece is ______ m.

______ m − ______ m = ______ m

The second piece is ______ m longer than the first piece.

6 Peter's mum spent £29·85 on food and £18·75 on drink. She paid the cashier £50. How much change did she get?

£ ____ + £ ____ = £ ____

The total cost of the food and drink is £ ____.

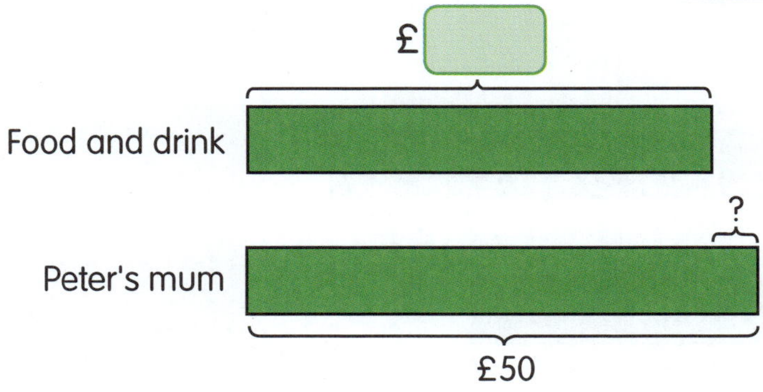

£ ____ − £ ____ = £ ____

She got £ ____ change.

7 Omar's dad went for a run on Monday and Tuesday. He ran 4·55 km on Monday and 1·78 km further on Tuesday than on Monday. What was the distance he ran on both days altogether?

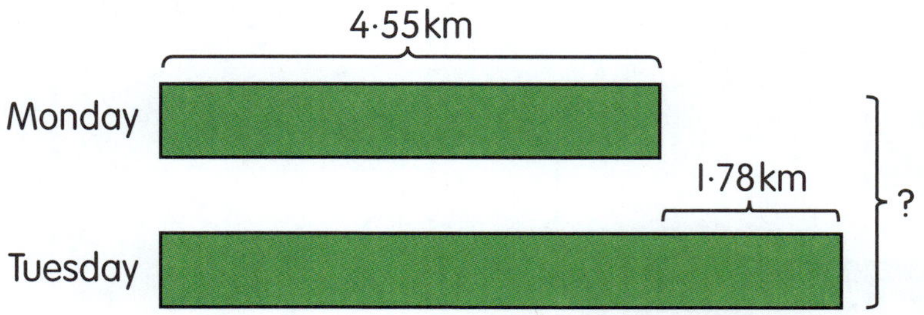

____ km + ____ km = ____ km

He ran ____ km on Tuesday.

____ km + ____ km = ____ km

He ran ____ km on both days altogether.

Practice Book 4B, p.47

Let's Learn!

Multiplication

1 Look at the number line below. Starting at the point zero, Tai moves 0·2 for each step he takes. Where will Tai be on the number line after 4 steps?

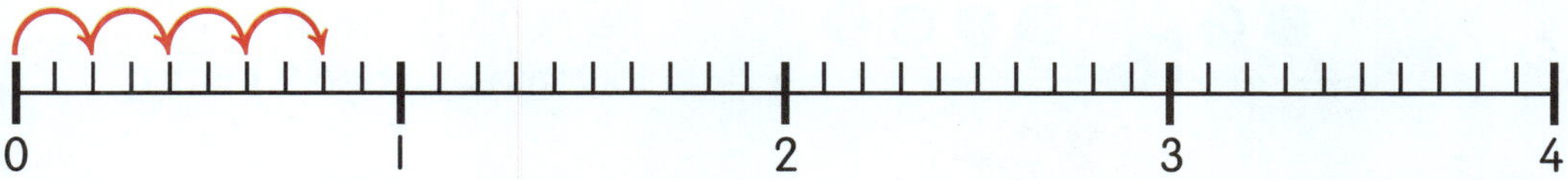

0·2 + 0·2 + 0·2 + 0·2 = 4 × 0·2
4 × 2 tenths = 8 tenths
= 0·8

After 4 steps, Tai will be at 0·8 on the number line.

2 Here is another way to multiply 0·2 by 4.

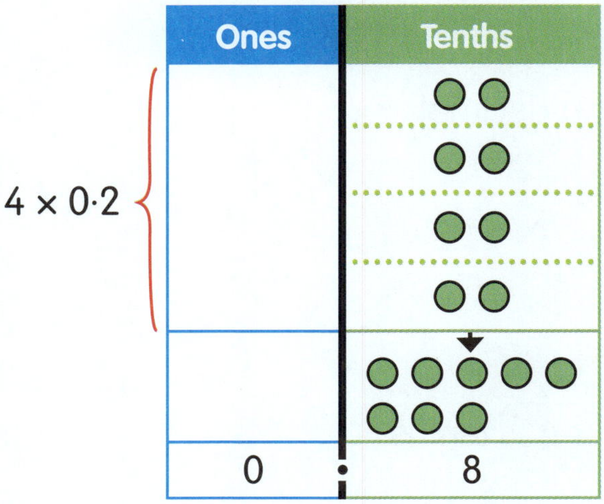

Multiply the **tenths** by 4.

$$\begin{array}{r} 0\cdot\mathbf{2} \\ \times \quad \mathbf{4} \\ \hline 0\cdot\mathbf{8} \\ \hline \end{array}$$

2 tenths × 4 = 8 tenths

So 4 × 0·2 = 0·8.

3 Multiply 2·4 by 3.

3 × 2·4

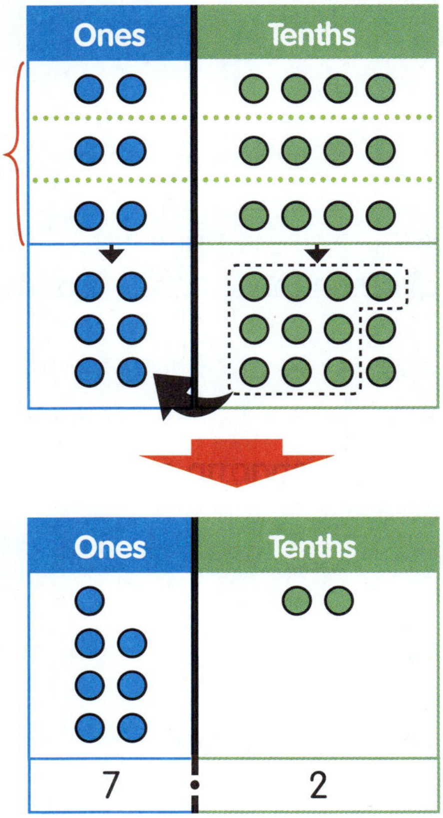

So 3 × 2·4 = 7·2.

First multiply the **tenths** by 3.

$$\begin{array}{r} 2\cdot\mathbf{4} \\ \times \quad \mathbf{3} \\ \hline \mathbf{2} \\ \hline {}_{1} \end{array}$$

4 tenths × 3 = 12 tenths

Regroup the tenths.
12 tenths = 1 one 2 tenths

Then multiply the **ones** by 3.

$$\begin{array}{r} \mathbf{2}\cdot 4 \\ \times \quad \mathbf{3} \\ \hline \mathbf{7}\cdot 2 \\ \hline {}_{1} \end{array}$$

2 ones × 3 = 6 ones

Add the ones.
6 ones + 1 one = 7 ones

4 Multiply and write the product as a decimal.

a 3 tenths × 2 = ☐ tenths
= ☐

b 6 tenths × 3 = ☐ tenths
= ☐ one ☐ tenths
= ☐

Home Maths

Encourage your child to multiply tenths or hundredths mentally. For example, to multiply 0·3 by 2, ask them to multiply 3 tenths by 2 mentally to get 6 tenths or 0·6. They can also use mental calculation for division.

5 Multiply.

a
$$\begin{array}{r} 0\cdot2 \\ \times\quad 3 \\ \hline \square \\ \hline \end{array}$$

b
$$\begin{array}{r} 0\cdot6 \\ \times\quad 8 \\ \hline \square \\ \hline \end{array}$$

c
$$\begin{array}{r} 3\cdot7 \\ \times\quad 7 \\ \hline \square \\ \hline \end{array}$$

6 Millie bought 3 rubbers for £0·45 each.
How much did she pay altogether?

£0·45 × 3 = ?

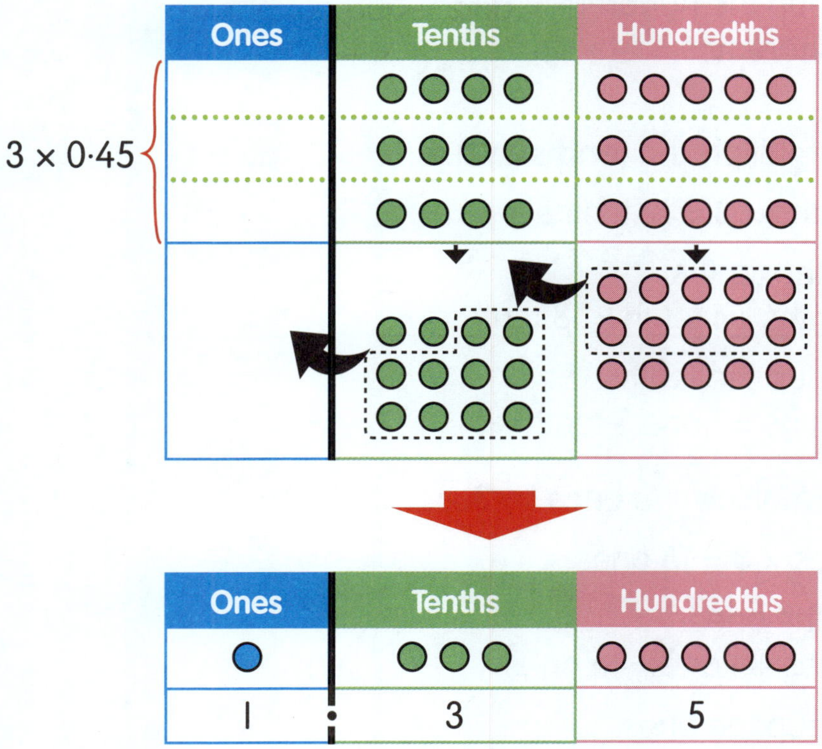

First multiply the **hundredths** by 3.

$$\begin{array}{r} 0\cdot4\mathbf{5} \\ \times\quad \mathbf{3} \\ \hline \mathbf{5} \\ \hline {\scriptstyle 1}\ \ \end{array}$$

5 hundredths × 3
= 15 hundredths

Regroup the hundredths.
15 hundredths
= 1 tenth 5 hundredths

Then multiply the **tenths** by 3.

$$\begin{array}{r} 0\cdot\mathbf{4}5 \\ \times\quad \mathbf{3} \\ \hline \mathbf{1}\cdot\mathbf{3}5 \\ \hline {\scriptstyle 1}\ \ \end{array}$$

4 tenths × 3 = 12 tenths

Add the tenths.
12 tenths + 1 tenth
= 13 tenths

Regroup the tenths.
13 tenths = 1 one 3 tenths

So £0·45 × 3 = £1·35.
She paid £1·35 altogether.

7 A large box of washing powder cost £15·45.
Millie's dad bought 3 of these boxes.
How much did he pay altogether?

£15·45 × 3 = ?

We multiply like this:

```
  1 5 · 4 5
×         3
-----------
          5
-----------
        1
```

First multiply the **hundredths** by 3.

5 hundredths × 3 = 15 hundredths

Regroup the hundredths.
15 hundredths = 1 tenth 5 hundredths

```
  1 5 · 4 5
×         3
-----------
      · 3 5
-----------
      1 1
```

Next multiply the **tenths** by 3.

4 tenths × 3 = 12 tenths

Add the tenths.
12 tenths + 1 tenth = 13 tenths

Regroup the tenths.
13 tenths = 1 one 3 tenths

```
  1 5 · 4 5
×         3
-----------
    6 · 3 5
-----------
    1 1   1
```

Then multiply the **ones** by 3.

5 ones × 3 = 15 ones

Add the ones.
15 ones + 1 one = 16 ones

Regroup the ones.
16 ones = 1 ten 6 ones

```
  1 5 · 4 5
×         3
-----------
  4 6 · 3 5
-----------
  1 1     1
```

Finally multiply the **tens** by 3.

1 ten × 3 = 3 tens

Add the tens.
3 tens + 1 ten = 4 tens

So £15·45 × 3 = £46·35.

He paid £46·35 altogether.

8 Multiply and write the product as a decimal.

a 6 hundredths × 4 = ☐ hundredths

= ☐ tenths ☐ hundredths

= ☐

b 7 hundredths × 3 = ☐ hundredths

= ☐ tenths ☐ hundredth

= ☐

9 Multiply.

a $0.03 \times 2 = \square$

b $0.07 \times 5 = \square$

c $0.65 \times 5 = \square$

d $2.08 \times 4 = \square$

e $2.16 \times 4 = \square$

f $3.14 \times 6 = \square$

g $1.05 \times 5 = \square$

h $6.95 \times 8 = \square$

i $31.78 \times 5 = \square$

10 Write in vertical form. Then multiply.

a £15·35 × 6

b 26·45 m × 4

c 1·76 kg × 5

d 18·25 m × 3

e 3·45 ℓ × 7

f £17·45 × 4

Practice Book 4B, p.49

Let's Learn!

Division

1 A ribbon that is 0·8 m long is cut into 2 equal pieces. How long is each piece?

0·8 ÷ 2 = ?

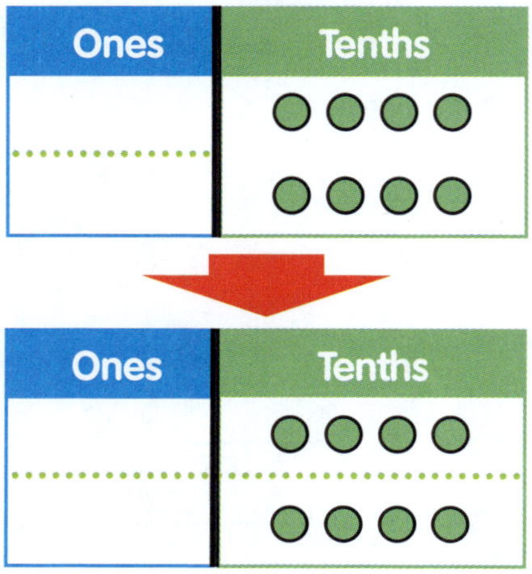

So 0·8 ÷ 2 = 0·4.
The length of each piece is 0·4 m.

First divide the **ones** by 2.
0 ones ÷ 2 = 0 ones

```
      0
2 ) 0·8
    0
    ---
```

Then divide the **tenths** by 2.
8 tenths ÷ 2 = 4 tenths

```
    0·4
2 ) 0·8
    0
    ---
      8
      8
    ---
      0
```

2 Divide 0·69 by 3.

Divide the **ones** by 3.	Divide the **tenths** by 3.	Divide the **hundredths** by 3.
3) 0·69 → 0; 0	3) 0·69 → 0·2; 0, 6, 6	3) 0·69 → 0·23; 0, 6, 6, 9, 9, 0
0 ones ÷ 3 = 0 ones	6 tenths ÷ 3 = 2 tenths	9 hundredths ÷ 3 = 3 hundredths

```
       0             0·2             0·23
3 ) 0·69        3 ) 0·69        3 ) 0·69
    0               0               0
    ----            ----            ----
                      6               6
                      6               6
                    ----            ----
                                        9
                                        9
                                     ----
                                        0
```

So 69 ÷ 3 = 0·23.

3 Divide.

a $2\overline{)\,0\cdot4}$ ☐

b $2\overline{)\,0\cdot26}$ ☐

c $3\overline{)\,0\cdot93}$ ☐

4 Divide 0·8 by 5.

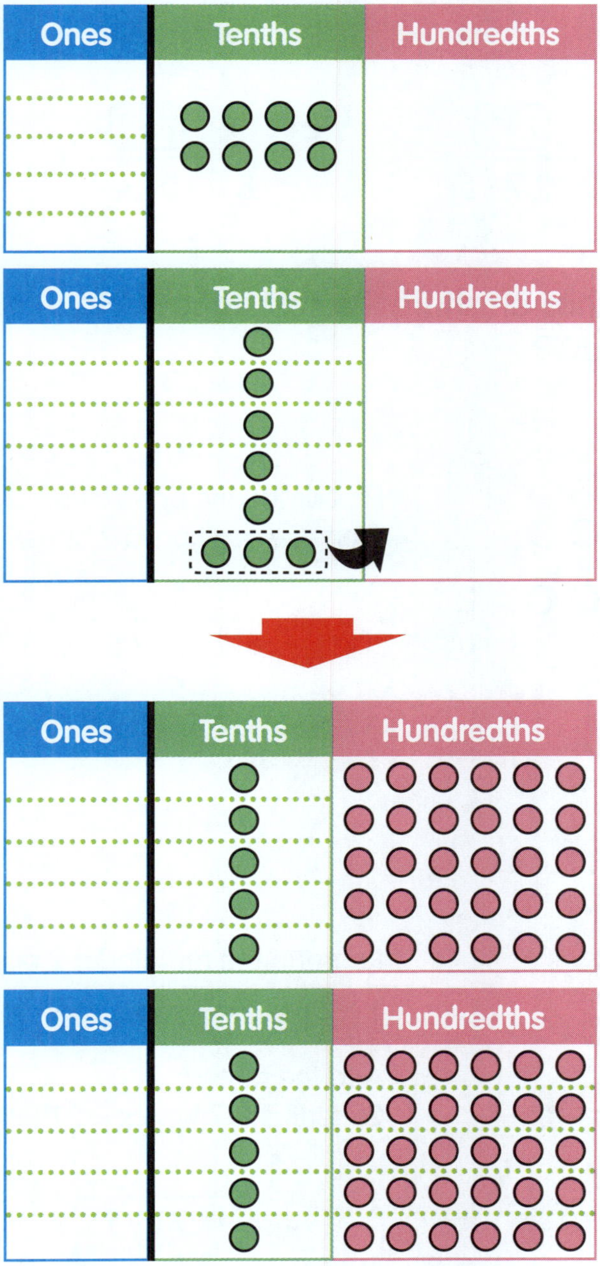

First divide the **ones** by 5.
0 ones ÷ 5 = 0 ones

```
     0
5 ) 0 · 8
    0
   ------
```

Then divide the **tenths** by 5.
8 tenths ÷ 5 = 1 tenth r 3 tenths

```
     0 · 1
5 ) 0 · 8
    0
   ------
        8
        5
   ------
        3
```

Regroup the remainder 3 tenths.
3 tenths = 30 hundredths

Finally divide the remainder 30 **hundredths** by 5.
30 hundredths ÷ 5
= 6 hundredths

```
     0 · 1 6
5 ) 0 · 8
    0
   --------
        8
        5
   --------
        3 0
        3 0
   --------
          0
```

So 0·8 ÷ 5 = 0·16.

5 Divide.

a 6 tenths ÷ 4 = ☐ tenth r ☐ tenths

b 2 tenths ÷ 4 = ☐ hundredths ÷ 4

= ☐ hundredths

6 Divide.

a ☐ 2) 0·9

b ☐ 5) 27·5

c ☐ 8) 0·4

7 A whole pizza costs £7·75. 5 children share the cost equally. How much will each pupil pay for their share?

£7·75 ÷ 5 = ?

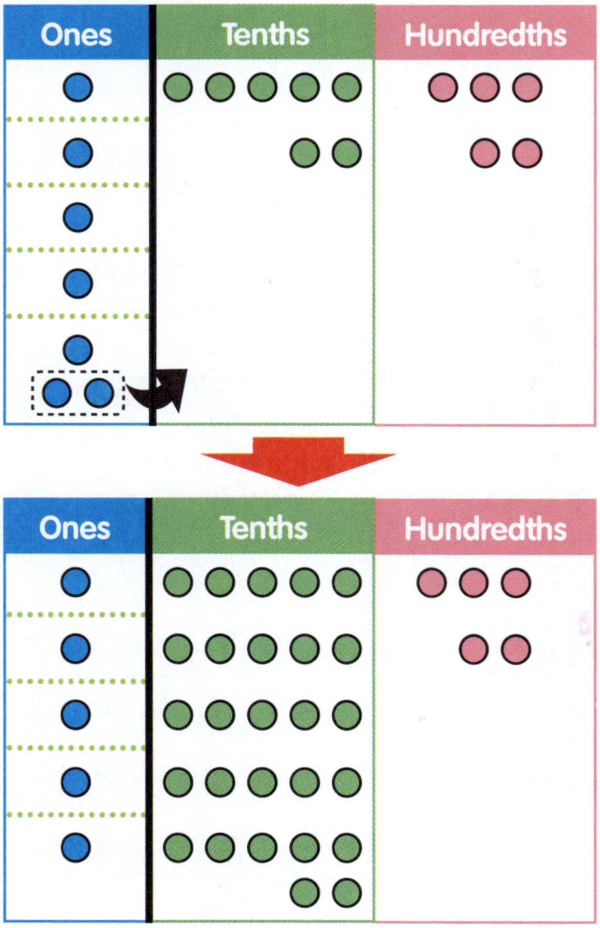

First divide the **ones** by 5.
7 ones ÷ 5 = 1 one r 2 ones

```
      1
5 ) 7·75
    5
    ---
    2
```

Regroup the remainder 2 ones.
2 ones = 20 tenths

Add the tenths.
20 tenths + 7 tenths = 27 tenths

```
      1
5 ) 7·75
    5
    ---
    2 7
```

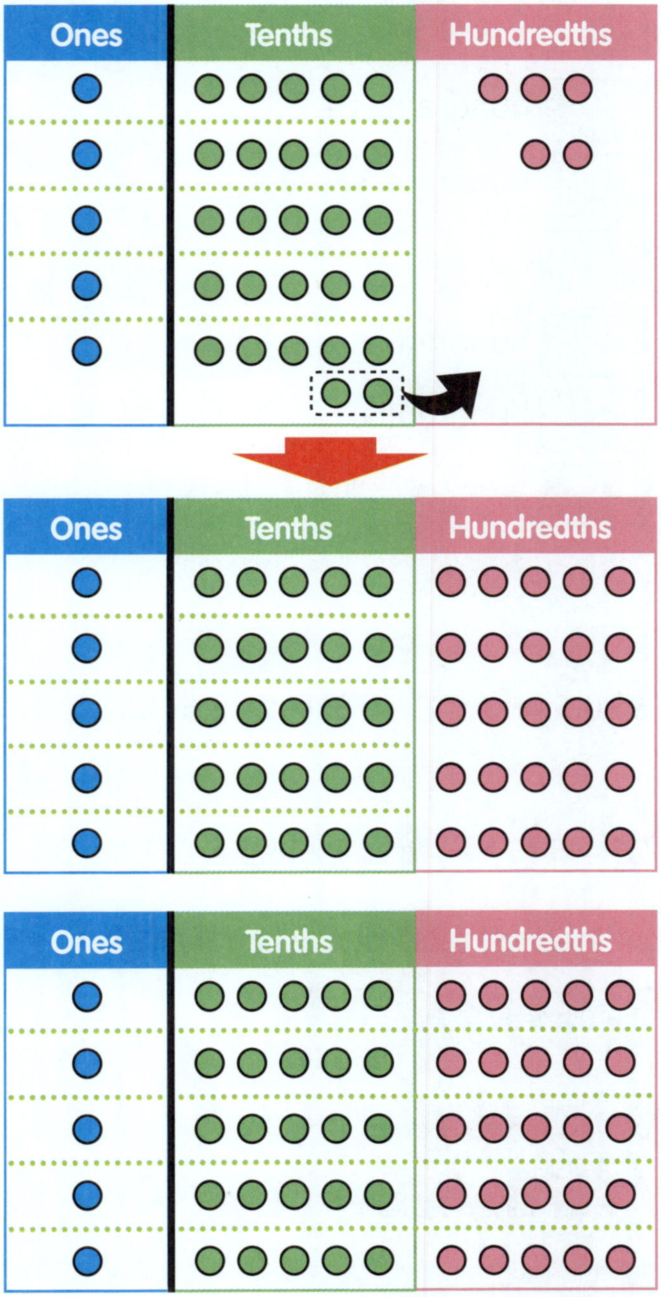

Then divide the **tenths** by 5.
27 tenths ÷ 5 = 5 tenths r 2 tenths

$$\begin{array}{r|l} & 1\cdot\mathbf{5}\ \ \\ \hline 5 & 7\cdot75 \\ & 5\ \ \ \ \ \\ \hline & 2\ 7\ \ \\ & \mathbf{2\ 5}\ \ \\ \hline & \mathbf{2}\ \ \end{array}$$

Regroup the remainder 2 tenths.
2 tenths = 20 hundredths

Add the hundredths.
20 hundredths + 5 hundredths
= 25 hundredths

$$\begin{array}{r|l} & 1\cdot5\ \ \\ \hline 5 & 7\cdot75 \\ & 5\ \ \ \ \ \\ \hline & 2\ 7\ \ \\ & 2\ 5\ \ \\ \hline & \mathbf{25} \end{array}$$

Finally divide the **hundredths** by 5.

$$\begin{array}{r|l} & 1\cdot5\mathbf{5} \\ \hline 5 & 7\cdot75 \\ & 5\ \ \ \ \ \\ \hline & 2\ 7\ \ \\ & 2\ 5\ \ \\ \hline & 25 \\ & \mathbf{25} \\ \hline & \mathbf{0} \end{array}$$

So £7·75 ÷ 5 = £1·55.

Each pupil will pay £1·55 for their share.

8 Regroup into hundredths. Then divide.

a 3 tenths 5 hundredths ÷ 7 = ☐ hundredths ÷ 7

= ☐ hundredths

= ☐

b 4 tenths 2 hundredths ÷ 6 = ☐ hundredths ÷ 6

= ☐ hundredths

= ☐

9 Divide.

a $2 \overline{)\, 0 \cdot 92}$ ☐

b $5 \overline{)\, 6 \cdot 05}$ ☐

c $3 \overline{)\, 2 \cdot 25}$ ☐

10 Divide.

a £7·40 ÷ 4 **b** £64·25 ÷ 5 **c** £26·95 ÷ 5

11 Find the value of 5 ÷ 8 correct to the nearest tenth or 1 decimal place.

```
    0·62
8 ) 5
    0
    ----
    5 0
    4 8
    ----
      20
      16
    ----
       4
```

5 ones ÷ 8 = 0 ones r 5 ones

Regroup the remainder 5 ones.
5 ones = 50 tenths
50 tenths ÷ 8 = 6 tenths r 2 tenths

Regroup the remainder 2 tenths.
2 tenths = 20 hundredths
20 hundredths ÷ 8
= 2 hundredths r 4 hundredths

Divide to 2 decimal places. Then round the answer to 1 decimal place.

0·62 is 0·6 when rounded to 1 decimal place.

5 ÷ 8 = 0·6 correct to 1 decimal place.

12 Find the value of 13 ÷ 8 correct to the nearest hundredth or 2 decimal places.

```
     1·625
8 ) 13
     8
     5 0
     4 8
      20
      16
       40
       40
        0
```

13 ones ÷ 8 = ___ one r ___ ones

Regroup the remainder 5 ones.
5 ones = 50 tenths
50 tenths ÷ 8 = ___ tenths r ___ tenths

Regroup the remainder 2 tenths.
2 tenths = 20 hundredths
20 hundredths ÷ 8
= ___ hundredths r ___ hundredths

Regroup the remainder 4 hundredths.
4 hundredths = 40 thousandths
40 thousandths ÷ 8 = ___ thousandths

Divide to 3 decimal places. Then round the answer to 2 decimal places.

1·625 is 1·63 when rounded to 2 decimal places.

13 ÷ 8 = 1·63 correct to 2 decimal places.

13 Regroup into tenths. Then divide.

a 2 ones ÷ 3 = ___ tenths ÷ 3
= ___ tenths r ___ tenths

b 4 ones ÷ 7 = ___ tenths ÷ 7
= ___ tenths r ___ tenths

14 Find the value of each of the following correct to the nearest tenth or 1 decimal place.

a $4\overline{)\,0\cdot7\,}$ = ☐

b $3\overline{)\,0\cdot56\,}$ = ☐

c $4\overline{)\,9\,}$ = ☐

15 Find the value of each of the following correct to the nearest tenth or 1 decimal place.

a $0{\cdot}8 \div 3$ **b** $0{\cdot}58 \div 4$ **c** $7 \div 9$

16 Find the value of each of the following correct to the nearest hundredth or 2 decimal places.

a $4\overline{)\,0\cdot78\,}$ = ☐

b $7\overline{)\,8\,}$ = ☐

c $6\overline{)\,10\,}$ = ☐

17 Find the value of each of the following correct to the nearest hundredth or 2 decimal places.

a $0{\cdot}3 \div 7$ **b** $0{\cdot}79 \div 2$ **c** $7 \div 6$

Practice Book 4B, p.53

Let's Learn!

Estimation of decimals

1 Estimate the value of £6·75 + £15·45 by rounding the amounts to the nearest pound.

£6·75 is £7 when rounded to the nearest pound.
£15·45 is £15 when rounded to the nearest pound.
£7 + £15 = £22
So £6·75 + £15·45 ≈ £22.

2 Estimate.

a 3·78 + 5·2 **b** 12·9 + 3·26 **c** 14·9 + 25·23

3 Calculate 31·65 + 8·02. Then check if your answer is reasonable using estimation.

Calculation

$$\begin{array}{r} 31\cdot65 \\ +\ \ 8\cdot02 \\ \hline 39\cdot67 \\ \hline \end{array}$$

Estimation

31·65 ≈ 32
8·02 ≈ 8

32 + 8 = 40

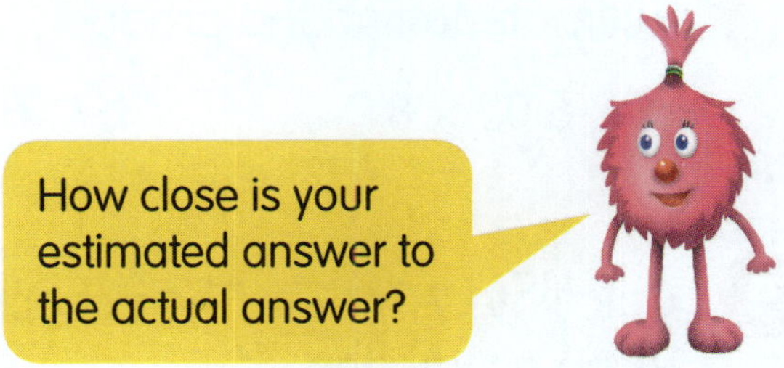

4 Estimate the value of 7·13 – 5·7 by rounding the numbers to the nearest whole number.

7·13 is 7 when rounded to the nearest whole number.
5·7 is 6 when rounded to the nearest whole number.
7 – 6 = 1
So the value of 7·13 – 5·7 ≈ 1.

5 Estimate to find the difference.

a 9·87 – 0·96 **b** 5·75 – 5·05 **c** 24·59 – 19·68

6 Calculate 11·09 – 1·86. Then check if your answer is reasonable using estimation.

Calculation

$$\begin{array}{r} 11.09 \\ -\ \ 1.86 \\ \hline 9.23 \end{array}$$

Estimation

11·09 ≈ 11
1·86 ≈ 2
11 – 2 = 9

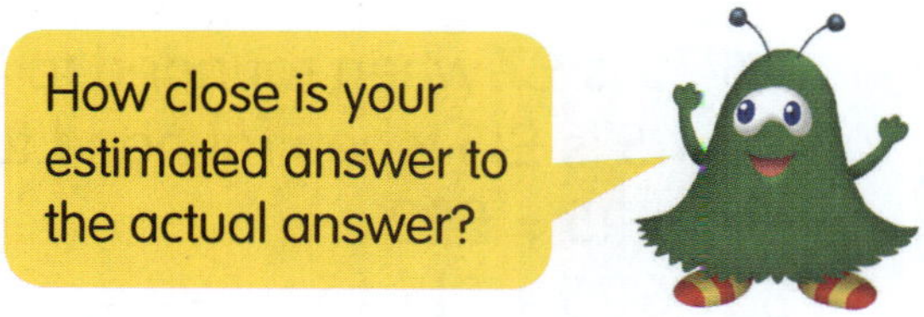

7 Estimate the value of 11·97 × 2 by rounding 11·97 to the nearest whole number.

11·97 is 12 when rounded to the nearest whole number.
12 × 2 = 24
So the value of 11·97 × 2 ≈ 24.

8 Estimate to find the product.

a 6·02 × 8 **b** 0·98 × 13 **c** 3·15 × 9

9 Calculate 2·74 × 4. Then check if your answer is reasonable using estimation.

Calculation

$$\begin{array}{r} 2.74 \\ \times\ \ \ \ 4 \\ \hline 10.96 \end{array}$$

Estimation

2·74 ≈ 3
3 × 4 = 12

10 Estimate the value of 23·64 ÷ 3.

23·64 → 21
23·64 → 24

Then divide.
24 ÷ 3 = 8
So the value of 23·64 ÷ 3 ≈ 8.

23·64 ÷ 3 → 21 ÷ 3
23·64 ÷ 3 → 24 ÷ 3
23·64 is closer to 24 than to 21.

11 Estimate to find the quotient.

a 12·3 ÷ 3 **b** 17·75 ÷ 9 **c** 20·99 ÷ 7

12 Calculate 40·4 ÷ 5. Then check if your answer is reasonable using estimation.

Calculation

```
     8 · 0 8
5 ) 4 0 · 4
    4 0
   ---------
        4
        0
   ---------
        4 0
        4 0
   ---------
          0
   ---------
```

Estimation

40·4 ≈ 40
40 ÷ 5 = 8

Use estimation to check that your answer is reasonable.

13 Estimate the value of 2·49 + 6·54 by rounding the numbers to the nearest tenth or 1 decimal place.

2·49 is 2·5 when rounded to the nearest tenth.
6·54 is 6·5 when rounded to the nearest tenth.
2·5 + 6·5 = 9
So 2·49 + 6·54 ≈ 9.

14 Estimate the value of each of the following.

a 10·16 – 3·78
10·16 is 10 when rounded to the nearest whole number.
3·78 is 4 when rounded to the nearest whole number.

10 – 4 = ____

So 10·16 – 3·78 ≈ ____.

b 0·47 × 4
0·47 is 0·5 when rounded to the nearest tenth.

0·5 × 4 = ____

So 0·47 × 4 ≈ ____.

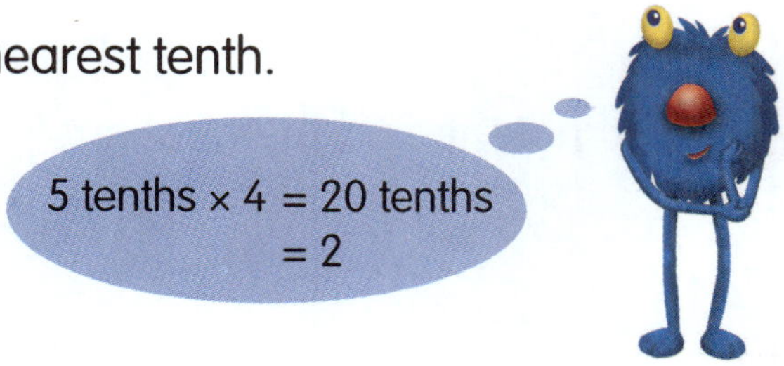

c **i** 3·46 ÷ 4

3·46 ÷ 4 → 3·2 ÷ 4
3·46 ÷ 4 → 3·6 ÷ 4

3·46 is nearer to 3·6 than to 3·2.

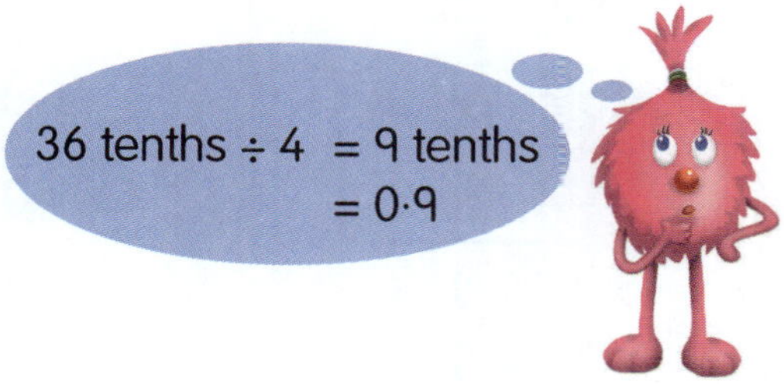

3·6 ÷ 4 = ____

So 3·46 ÷ 4 ≈ ____.

ii 5·28 ÷ 6

5·28 ÷ 6 → 4·8 ÷ 6
5·28 ÷ 6 → 5·4 ÷ 6

5·28 is nearer to 5·4 than to 4·8.

5·4 ÷ 6 = ____

So 5·28 ÷ 6 ≈ ____.

15 Calculate. Then check if your answer is reasonable using estimation.

a £12·42 + £12·64 **b** £1·45 – £0·54

c £1·79 × 3 **d** £1·45 ÷ 5

Home Maths Encourage your child to use estimation to check if the answers they have given seem reasonable. By rounding numbers they can make the calculations easier to check.

Practice Book 4B, p.59

Let's Learn!

Word problems

1 A pile of 7 identical maths books is 4·55 cm high. Find the height of 9 of these books. Round your answer to 1 decimal place.

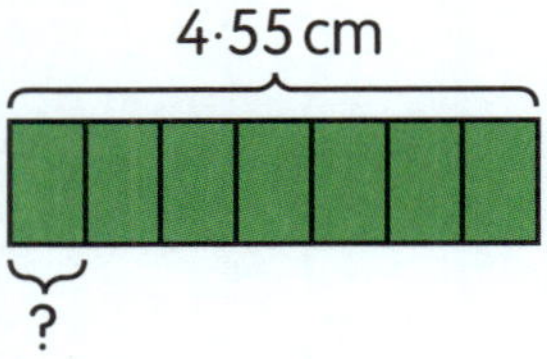

4·55 ÷ 7 = 0·65

The height of 1 maths book is 0·65 cm.

0·65 × 9 = 5·85

5·85 is 5·9 when rounded to 1 decimal place.

The height of 9 maths books is about 5·9 cm.

2 Miya saved £12·15. Jack saved 3 times as much money as Miya. Ella saved £24·50 less than Jack. How much money did Ella save?

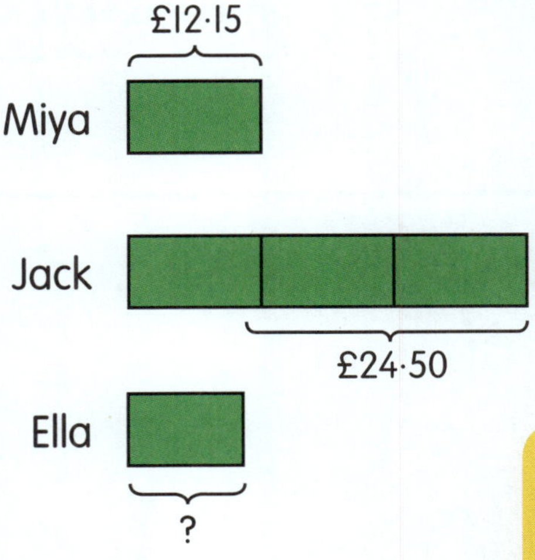

☐ × £12·15 = £☐

Jack saved £☐.

£☐ – £24·50 = £☐

Ella saved £☐.

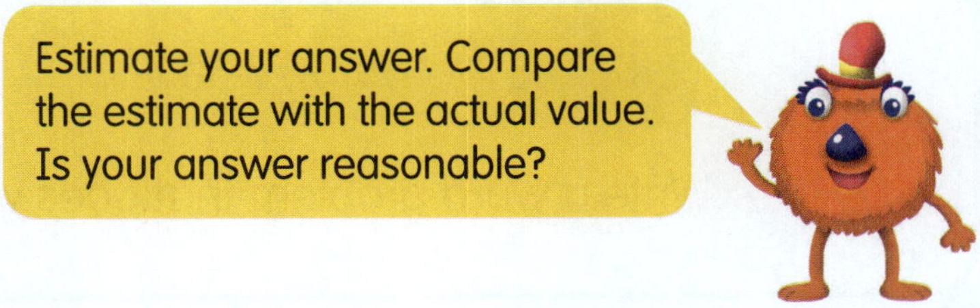

3 Mrs Thomas wants to buy 3 watches that cost £69·65 each.
Estimate the least number of £5 notes she needs to buy the watches.

£69·65 ≈ £____

3 × £____ = £____

Total cost of 3 watches ≈ £____

____ ÷ 5 = ____

She needs ____ £5 notes.

4 A wooden vase and 4 identical glass vases have a total mass of 21·6 kg.
The mass of the wooden vase is 3·3 kg. What is the mass of each glass vase? Round your answer to 2 decimal places.

21·6 − 3·3 = ____

The total mass of 4 identical glass vases is ____ kg.

____ ÷ 4 ≈ ____

The mass of each glass vase is ____ kg.

Practice Book 4B, p.63

Activity

5 **a** Ruby wrote these sentences.

2 × £11·20 = £22·40

£100 − £22·40 = £77·60

Write a word problem that goes with these sentences.

Activity

b Omar wrote the following sentences.

$24{\cdot}15\text{ kg} - 6{\cdot}45\text{ kg} = 17{\cdot}7\text{ kg}$

$17{\cdot}7\text{ kg} \div 3 = 5{\cdot}9\text{ kg}$

Write a word problem that goes with these sentences.

Let's Explore!

6 Peter has some five pence and twenty pence coins. The total amount Peter has is £1·15. How many five pence and twenty pence coins could he have?

Maths Journal

7 Use the information below to write one word problem. Then solve it.

Put On Your Thinking Caps!

8 **a** Arrange the numbers below in the circles so that the sum of the three numbers along each line is 4·5.

1·2 1·8 1·4 1·6 1·5

(Hint: The sum of the opposite numbers is the same as the sum of the other two opposite numbers.)

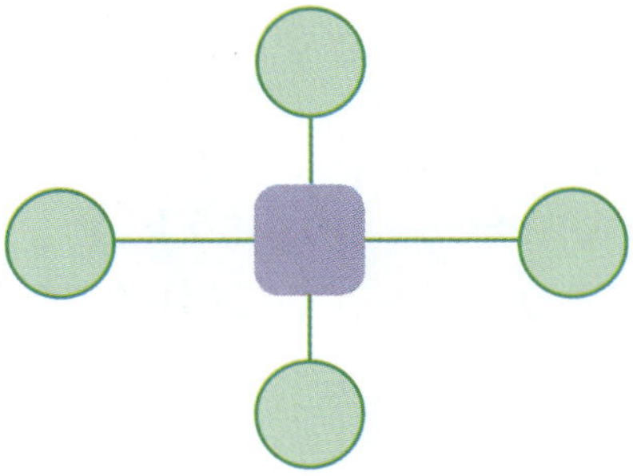

b The number in the square is the product of the numbers in the two circles next to it. Find the numbers in the circles.

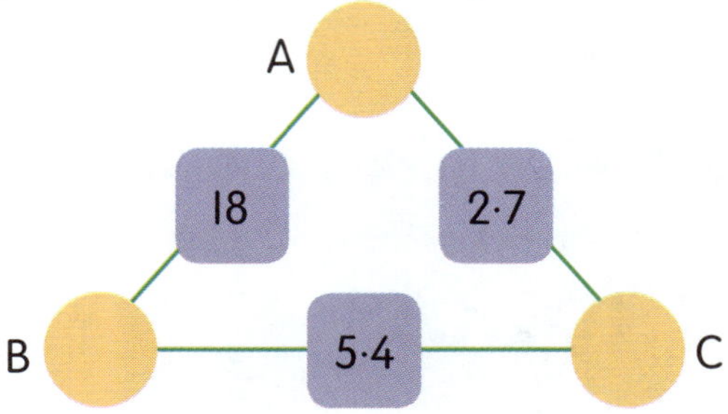

Practice Book 4B, p.67

Practice Book 4B, p.68

Unit 11 Time

Let's Learn!

Seconds

1

This is the **second hand**.

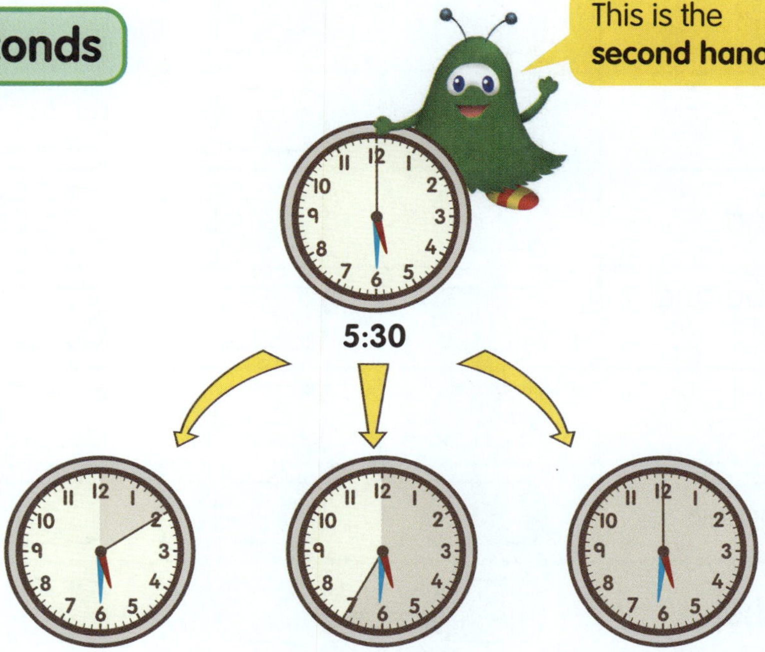

10 seconds later | 35 seconds later | 60 seconds later

One complete turn round the clock by the second hand is equal to 60 seconds.

60 seconds = 1 minute

The **second** is another unit of measurement for time. We use **s** to stand for seconds.

2

Farha, what can you do in 1 s?

Wow! That was fast!

I can say, one thousand and one!

Activity

3 Does each activity below take 1 s, more than 1 s or less than 1 s?

Activity	1 s	More Than 1 s	Less Than 1 s
Say "thirty-four"			
Blink once			
Raise your hand			
Raise your hand and bring it down			
Nod twice			
Say your full name			
Say the alphabet			

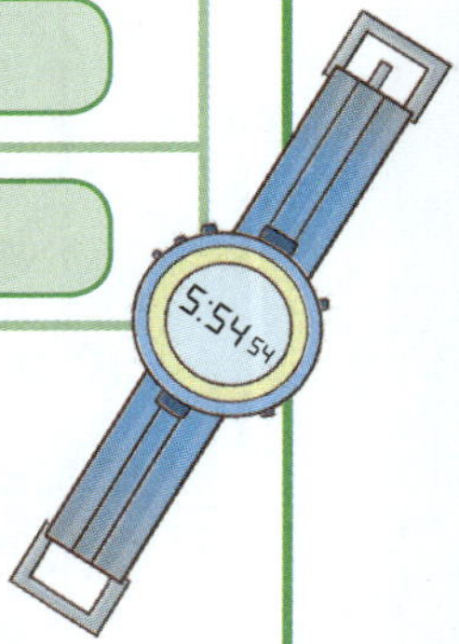

4 Jack walks from one end of the classroom to the other. Ruby times him.

Jack takes 10 s to walk from one end of the classroom to the other.

Game

Players: 2

You will need:
- 2 containers, A and B
- 30 marbles
- stopwatch

5 How to play:

1 Player 1 puts 10 marbles into Container A.

2 Player 1 takes the marbles out of Container A one at a time and puts them into Container B as fast as they can.

3 Player 2 draws up a table as shown below. Player 2 estimates the time Player 1 will take to transfer the 10 marbles. Player 2 writes down the estimate in the table.

4 Player 2 uses a stopwatch and times Player 1 as Player 1 transfers the 10 marbles. Player 2 records the actual time taken in the table.

5 Players 1 and 2 repeat steps **1** to **4** for transferring 20 marbles and 30 marbles.

6 The players then swap roles and repeat the game.

Player 1		
Number of Marbles Transferred	**Time Taken in Seconds to Transfer Marbles**	
	Estimate	**Actual**
10		
20		
30		
Total Time Taken		

The winner is the player whose estimates are closest to the actual times.

6

The clock shows 8:20.

After 60 s, the time is ______.

Another 60 s later, the time is ______.

7 Find the duration.

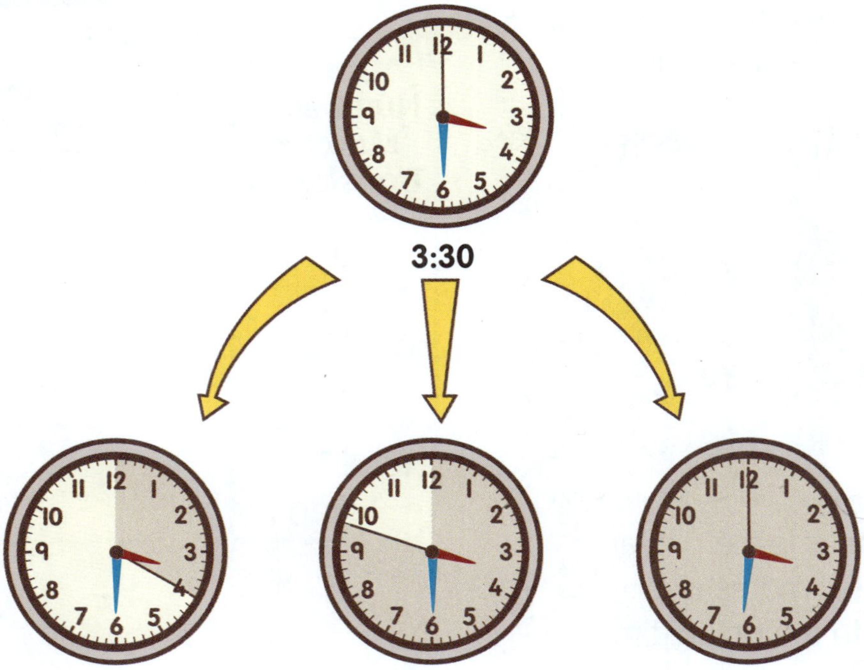

______ s later   ______ s later   ______ s later

8 You will need some clock faces. Draw the missing minute and/or second hand(s) on each clock face. Then find out the time.

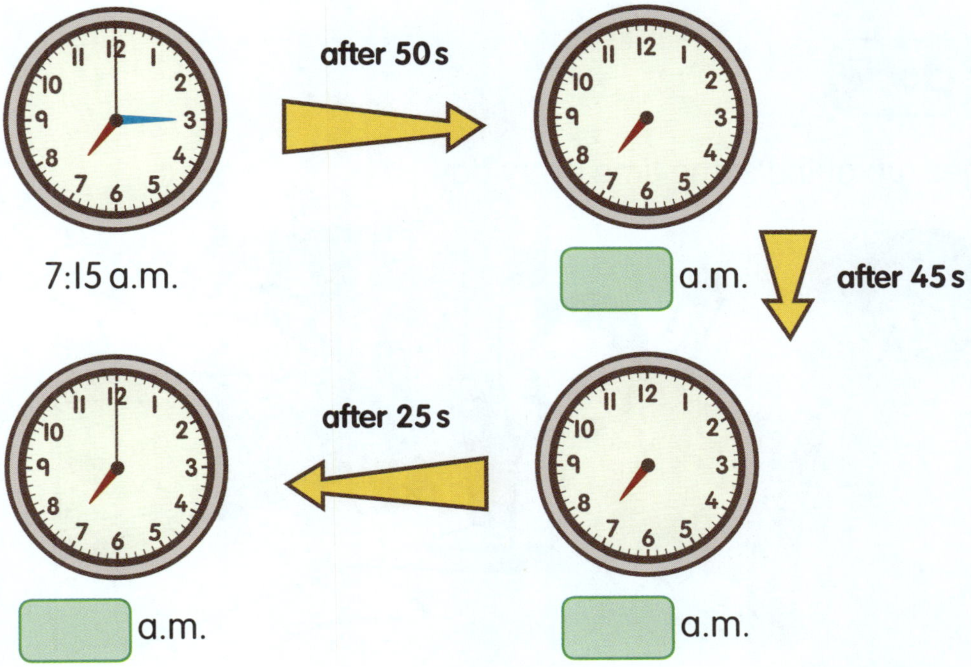

Activity

9

1. You have 60 s to make a paper aeroplane.
2. Did you make the plane in 60 s or less?
3. Next, throw the paper aeroplane into the air and work in pairs to count the number of seconds before it falls to the ground.
   One person counts using "thousands" like this:
   Each "thousand" stands for one second.
   The other uses a stopwatch.
4. How many seconds did the paper aeroplane stay in the air? Compare your answers.

Practice Book 4B, p.79

Let's Learn!

24-hour clock

1 Miya gets up at the same time every day.

Look at the time on the clock.

It is 7:30 in the morning. We write it as **7:30 a.m.**
We read it as **seven thirty a.m.**

We can write the time in another way.

We can write it as **07:30**.
We read it as **zero seven thirty hours**.

7:30 a.m. is a way of showing time using the 12-hour clock.

07:30 is a way of showing time using the 24-hour clock.

2 School starts at 9:00 in the morning every day.

a Using the 12-hour clock, we write the time as ____.

b Using the 24-hour clock, we write the time as ____.

3 Write the following times using the 24-hour clock.

a 9:15 a.m. **b** 11:05 a.m.

4 Write the following times using the 12-hour clock.

a 08:45 **b** 10:24

5 School ends at 3:20 in the afternoon every day.
We write the time as 3:20 p.m.

3:20 p.m. is expressing the time using the 12-hour clock.

How do we express 3:20 p.m. using the 24-hour clock?

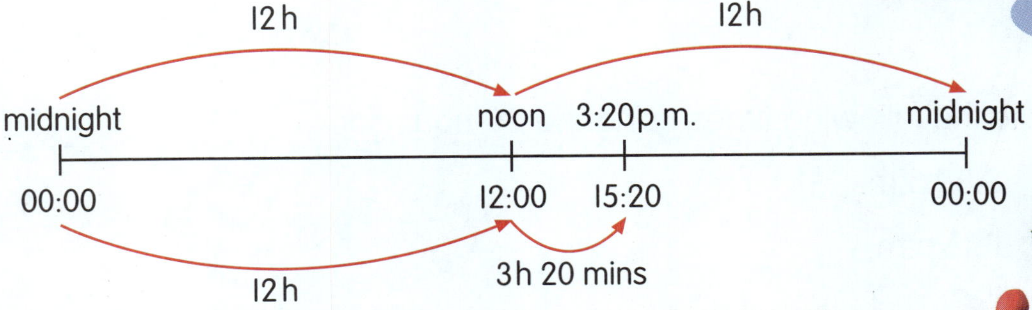

12 + 3 = 15

We can also say that school ends at 15:20 every day.

We read 15:20 as **fifteen twenty hours**.

Home Maths

Explain to your child that in the 24-hour clock, midnight is represented by 00:00. Using a time line, explain to your child.

To convert 1:45 p.m. to 13:45

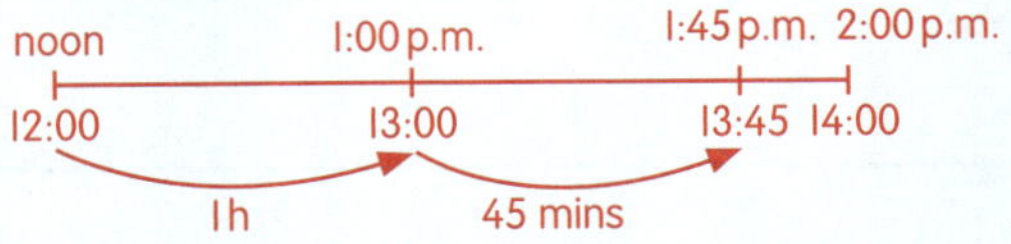

6 Miya goes to bed at 9:00 every night. We write the time as 9:00 p.m.

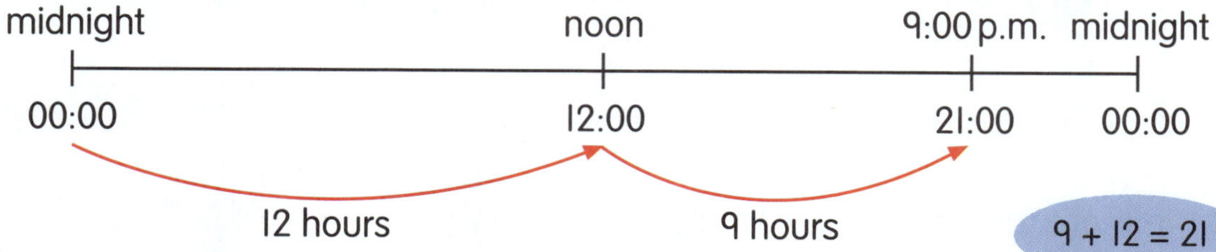

9 + 12 = 21

21:00 is another way of showing 9:00 p.m.
Miya goes to bed at 21:00 every night.

We read 21:00 as **twenty-one hundred hours**

7 Write the following times using the 24-hour clock.

a 8:30 p.m.

b 11:15 p.m.

a Add ☐ to ☐.
b Add ☐ to ☐.

Home Maths

Help your child to draw a time line for a 12-hour clock and a 24-hour clock (a guide on how to do this is given below). Then ask your child to tell the time using the time line for the 24-hour and 12-hour clocks.

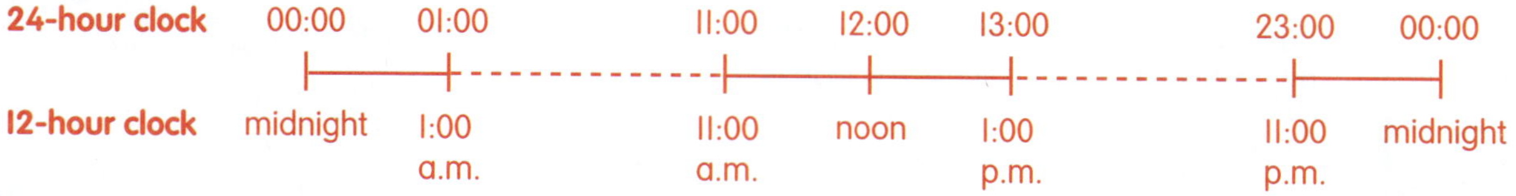

8 What is 21:35 using the 12-hour clock?

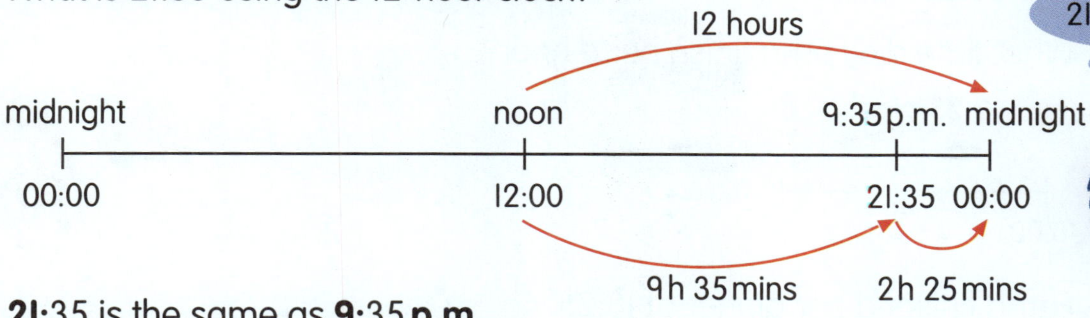

21:35 is the same as 9:35 p.m.

Using the 12-hour clock, 21:35 is 9:35 p.m.

9 Express the following times using the 24-hour clock.

a 8:50 a.m. **b** 8:50 p.m.

c 6:30 a.m. **d** 9:15 a.m.

e 7:40 p.m. **f** 11:25 p.m.

10 Express the following times using the 12-hour clock.

a 07:35 **b** 19:35

c 08:20 **d** 12:30

e 18:40 **f** 21:35

11 Millie started tidying her room at 16:00. She finished tidying at 16:35. How long did it take Millie to tidy her room?

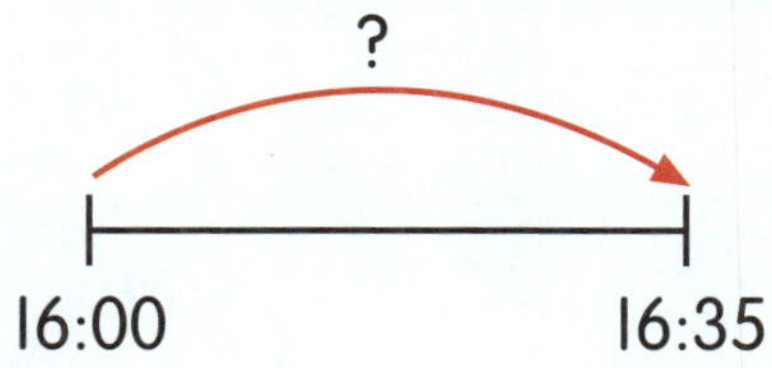

Millie took 35 mins to tidy her room.

12 Farha had her dinner at 18:00. She finished her dinner 25 minutes later. What time did Farha finish her dinner?

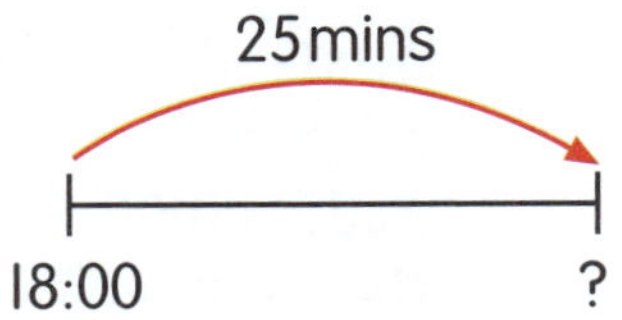

Farha finished her dinner at 18:25.

13 Ella finished her piano lesson at 15:45. Her lesson lasted 40 minutes. What time did Ella begin her piano lesson?

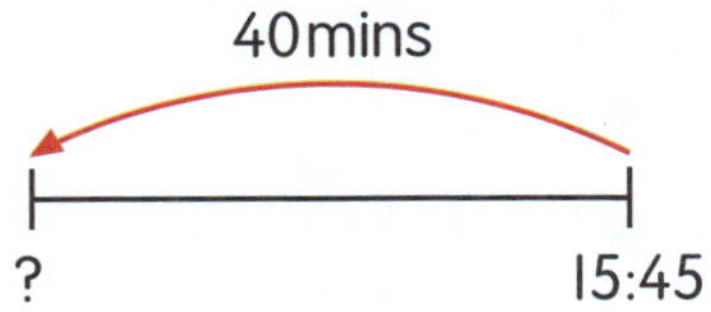

Ella began her piano lesson at 15:05.

14 Ben left the cinema at 19:45. He took a bus and got home 50 minutes later. What time did Ben get home?

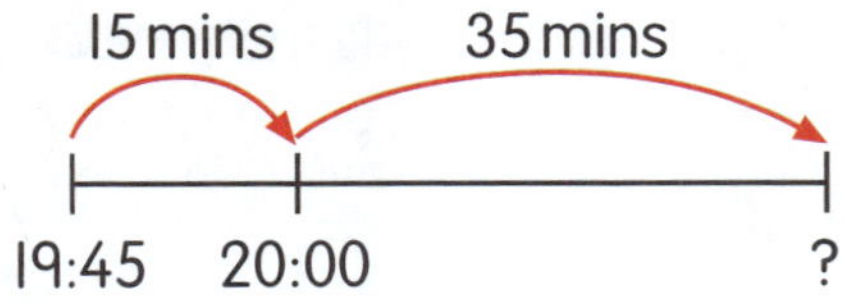

Ben got home at 20:35.

15 Miya began painting a picture at 12:25. She finished painting the picture 45 minutes later. What time did Miya finish painting the picture?

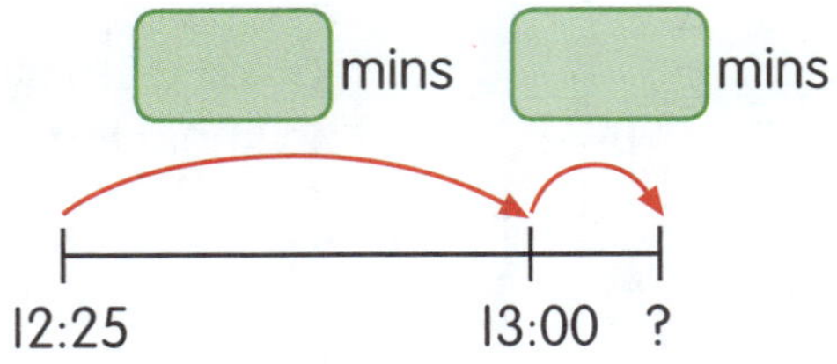

Miya finished painting the picture at ______.

16 Peter's dad baked a cake in the oven for 50 minutes. He removed the cake from the oven at 10:15. What time did Peter's dad start baking?

50 mins = 15 mins + ____ mins

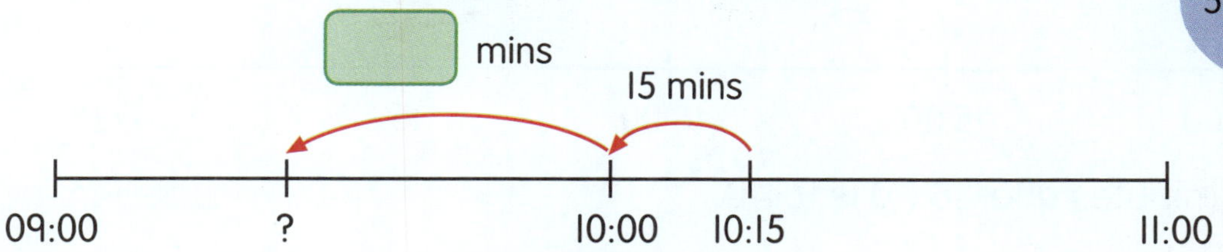

Peter's dad started baking at ____.

17 A music concert started at 19:45. It ended at 21:20. How long did the music concert last?

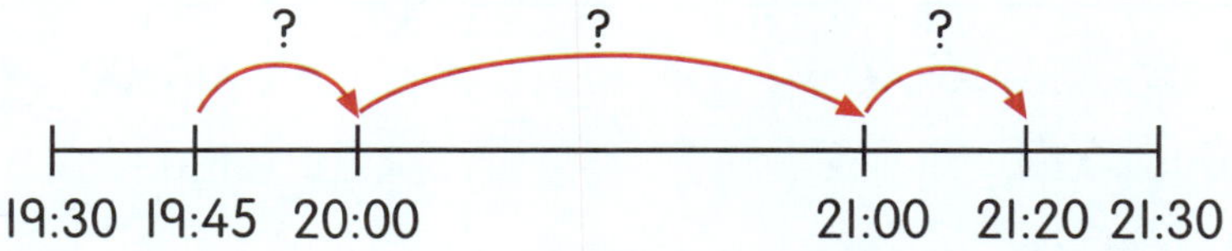

The concert lasted ____ h ____ mins.

18 Omar took 40 minutes to write a short story. He started writing at 11:45. What time did he finish writing?

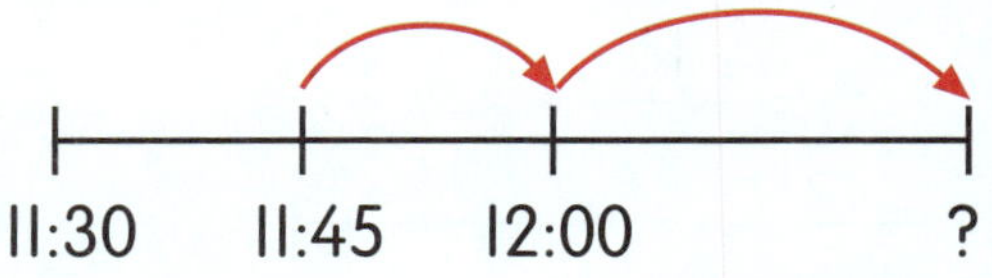

He finished writing at ____.

19 Sophia took a train from London Paddington station and reached Heathrow Central station 26 minutes later. She arrived at Heathrow Central station at 11:20. What time did she board the train at London Paddington station?

She boarded the train at ____.

20 Tai's art lesson started at 15:30. The lesson lasted 1 h 10 mins. What time did the art lesson end?

Method 1

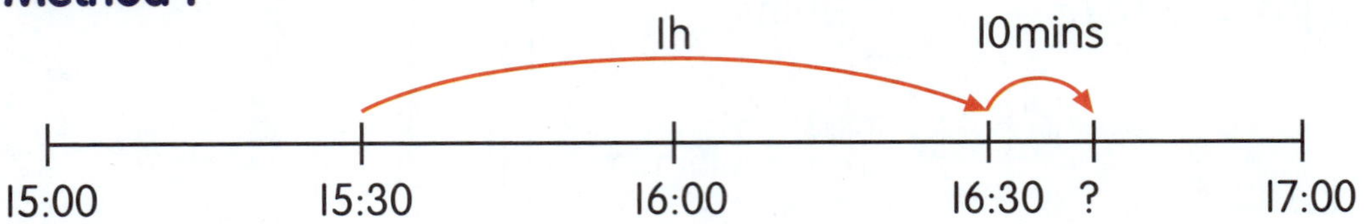

10 minutes after 16:30 is 16:40.

Method 2

1 h 10 mins = 70 mins = 30 mins + 40 mins

40 minutes after 16:00 is 16:40.

The art lesson ended at 16:40.

21 A film ended at 22:05. It lasted 2 h 25 mins. What time did the film start?

Method 1

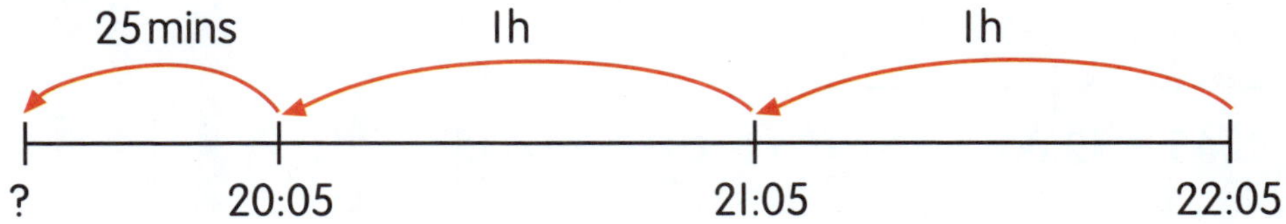

Method 2

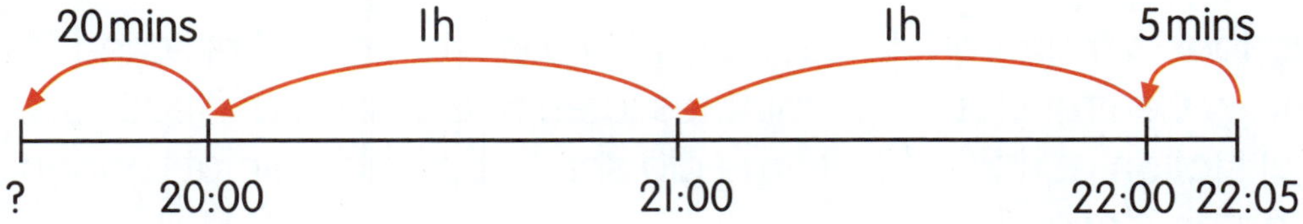

The film started at ______.

Home Maths

You can help your child to become more familiar with 24-hour clock times by looking at bus or train timetables together. Encourage your child to use the timetables to work out when a bus or train is due.

22 A train left Birmingham at 13:45 and arrived in London at 15:10 on the same day. How long was the journey?

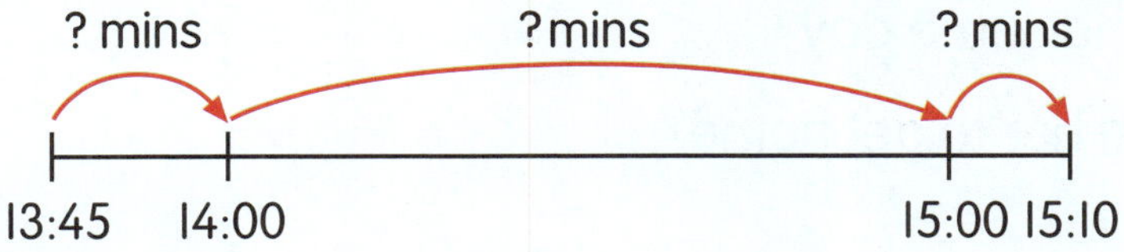

From	**To**	**Time Taken**
13:45	14:00	15 mins
14:00	15:00	60 mins = 1 h
15:00	15:10	10 mins
	Total time	1 h 25 mins

The journey was 1 h 25 mins long.

23 Omar's dad started running at 17:45 and finished at 19:15. How long did he run for?

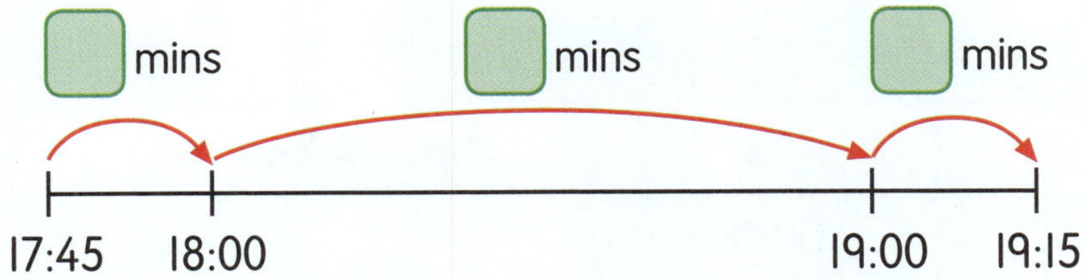

From	**To**	**Time Taken**
17:45	18:00	
18:00	19:00	
19:00	19:15	
	Total time	

He ran for ____ h ____ mins.

24 Ruby's aunt went to see a band on Saturday. The band finished playing at 23:30. Ruby's aunt got home at 00:15.

a Did she get home the same day?

b How long did it take her to get home?

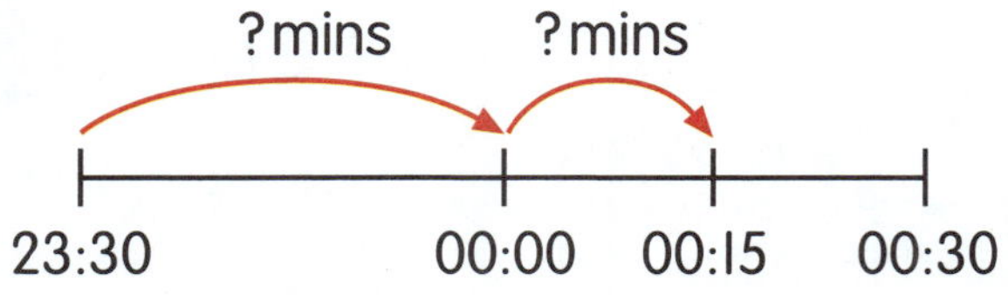

a

Midnight is written as 00:00. 00:15 is after midnight. Ruby's aunt got home on Sunday!

b

From	To	Time Taken
23:30	00:00 (end of Saturday)	30 mins
00:00 (beginning of Sunday)	00:15	15 mins
	Total time	45 mins

It took Ruby's aunt 45 mins to get home.

25 A train left Paddington station at 22:50 on Wednesday. It arrived in Cardiff at 01:20. How long was the journey? Did the train reach Cardiff on the same day or the next day?

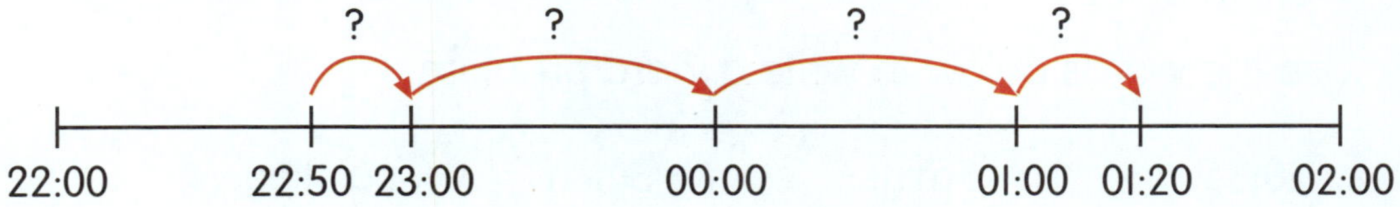

From	To	Time Taken
22:50	23:00	
23:00	00:00	
00:00	01:00	
01:00	01:20	

The journey was ☐ h ☐ mins long.

The train reached Cardiff the ☐ day.

Maths Journal

26 Using the 24-hour clock, make a diary of your activities on a school day from the time you get up to the time you go to bed.

Example

Activity

27 Work in pairs.

a Use the words below to write a word problem.

20:35	1 h 45 mins	Mr Smith	painting
began	finished	what time	he took

Exchange word problems with your partner and try to solve them.

b The table below shows the departure times of trains from London stations and their arrival times at various destinations in the UK.

Destination	Time of Departure From London	Expected Time of Arrival at Destination
Leicester	08:05	09:30
Eastbourne	13:25	14:50
Brighton	15:10	16:05
York	17:05	19:30
Northampton	18:35	20:00

i How long does it take to go from London to Leicester?

ii June took the train from London to Brighton. June's mother took a later train and arrived in Brighton at 21:35. Her journey took the same amount of time as June's. What time did the train that her mother took depart from London?

iii Mr Lim took the train to York. His train was delayed for 45 minutes. What time did Mr Lim finally arrive in York?

iv Miss Bell was on the train to Eastbourne when she was told that due to bad weather, they would be arriving in Eastbourne later than expected. She finally arrived in Eastbourne at 15:15. How long was the journey?

Practice Book 4B, p.81

Maths Journal

28 The list below shows what has been covered in this unit. Write down which parts of this unit you like the most and which parts you find difficult.

24-hour clock:

a Change time from 12-hour clock to 24-hour clock.

b Change time from 24-hour clock to 12-hour clock.

c Find duration.

d Find the end time.

e Find the start time.

Put On Your Thinking Caps!

29 Mr Green got off a train at 00:30 on Saturday. His journey was 55 minutes long. At what time did he get on board the train? What day was it?

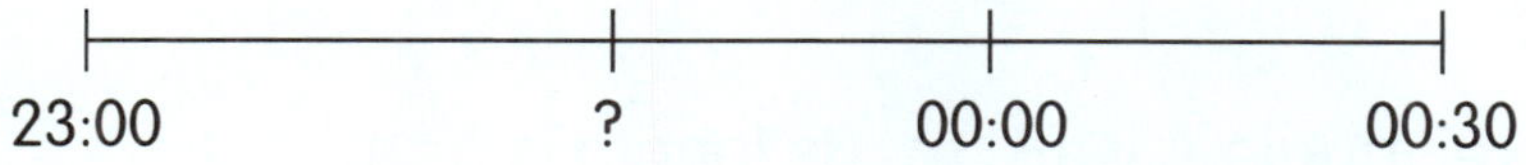

Mr Green got on the train at ______. It was ______.

Practice Book 4B, p.87

Practice Book 4B, p.88

Unit 12 Area and Perimeter

Let's Learn!

Rectangles and squares

Perimeter

1

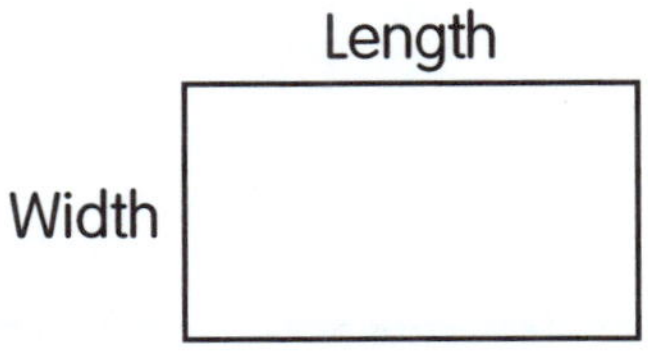

Perimeter of rectangle = Length + Width + Length + Width
= Length of all its 4 sides

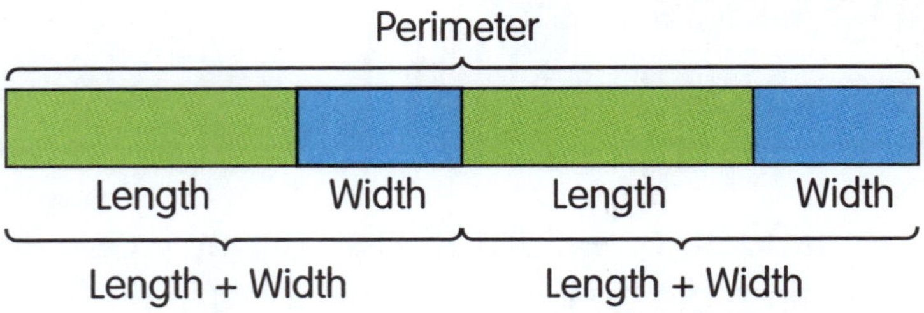

Length + Width of a rectangle is equal to $\frac{1}{2}$ of its perimeter.

2 The perimeter of Rectangle A is 18 cm. Its length is 6 cm. Find its width.

Rectangle A

Perimeter = 18 cm
Length + Width = Perimeter ÷ 2
= 18 ÷ 2
= 9 cm

6 cm + Width = 9 cm
Width = 9 − 6 = 3 cm

The width of Rectangle A is 3 cm.

3 The perimeter of Rectangle B is 28 cm. Its length is 8 cm. Find its width.

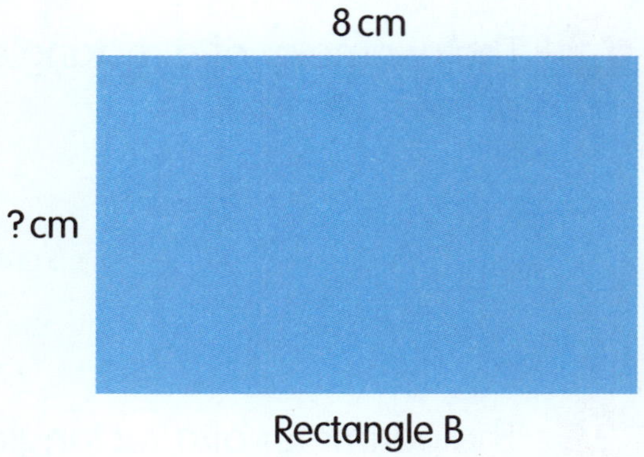

Length + Width = Perimeter ÷ 2
= ____ ÷ ____
= ____ cm

8 cm + Width = ____ cm
Width = ____ − ____
= ____ cm

The width of Rectangle B is ____ cm.

4 The perimeter of a square is 64 cm. Find the length of a side of the square.

All the sides of a square are equal.
There are 4 sides in a square.
Length of a side = Perimeter ÷ 4
= 64 ÷ 4
= 16 cm

The length of a side of the square is 16 cm.

5 Abby bent a piece of wire 132 cm long into a square. What is the length of a side of the square?

Length of a side = ____ ÷ 4 = ____ cm

The length of a side of the square is ____ cm.

6 The perimeter of a rectangle is 32 cm. Its width is 5 cm. Find the length of the rectangle.

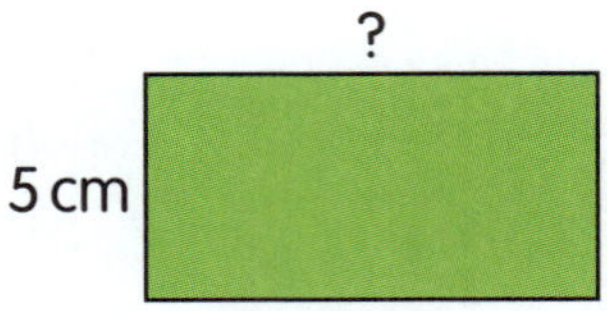

7 The perimeter of a rectangle is 128 cm. Its length is 35 cm. Find the width of the rectangle.

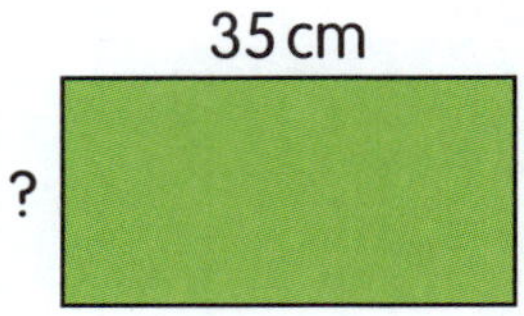

8 The perimeter of a square is 36 cm. Find the length of one side of the square.

9 Jack stuck a ribbon of length 72 cm around a box with a square top. What is the length of one side of the square top?

10 Millie walks 480 m around a rectangular field once. The length of the field is 160 m. What is the width of the field?

Practice Book 4B, p.89

Area

11

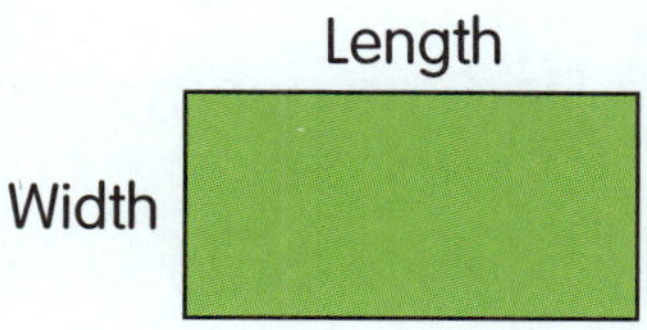

Area of rectangle = Length × Width

or

Length × Width = Area of rectangle

12 The area of a rectangular carpet is 63 m^2.
Its length is 9 m. Find its width.

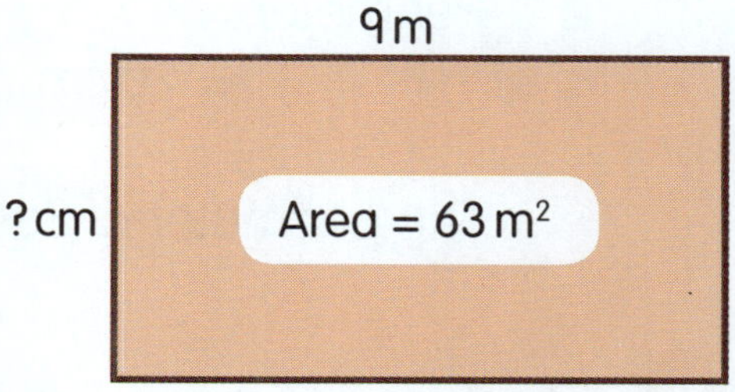

Area = 63 m^2, Length = 9 m

Length × Width = Area

9 m × Width = 63 m^2

Width = 63 ÷ 9

= 7 m

Its width is 7 m.

13 The area of a rectangular piece of land is 96 m^2.
Its width is 8 m. Find its length.

Area = ____ m^2, Width = ____ m

Length × ____ = ____ m^2

Length = ____ ÷ ____

= ____ m

Its length is ____ m.

14 The area of Square A is 25 cm^2.

a Find the length of a side of the square.

b Find the perimeter of the square.

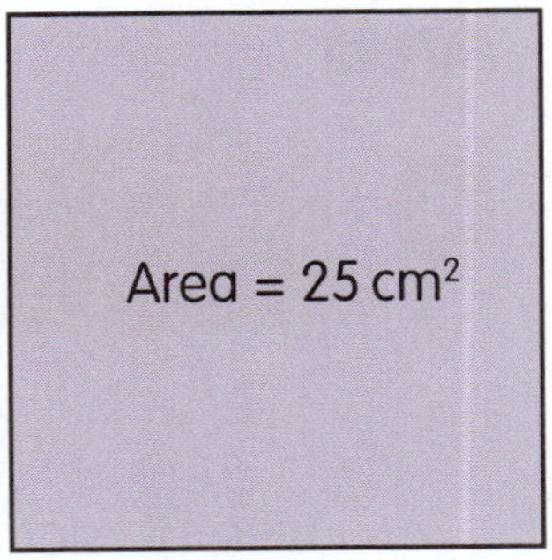

Square A

a Area = 25 cm^2

25 = 5 × 5

Length of side = 5 cm

The length of a side of Square A is 5 cm.

b Perimeter = 4 × 5

= 20 cm

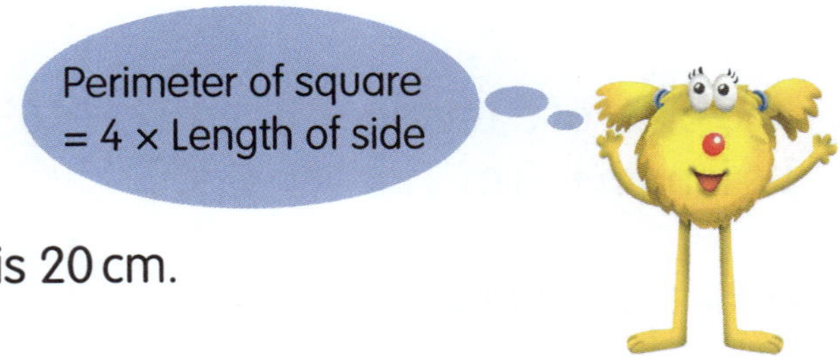

The perimeter of Square A is 20 cm.

15 The area of Square B is 49 cm^2.

a Find the length of a side of the square.

b Find the perimeter of the square.

a Area = 49 cm^2

49 = ______ × ______

Length = ______ cm

The length of a side of Square B is ______ cm.

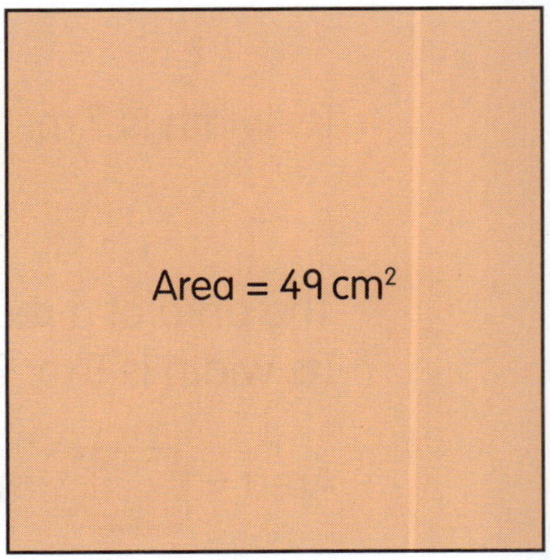

Square B

b Perimeter = 4 × ______

= ______ cm

The perimeter of Square B is ______ cm.

16 The area of a rectangular garden is 48 m^2. Its length is 8 m. Find its width.

17 The area of a square tile is 81 cm^2. Find the length of a side of the square tile.

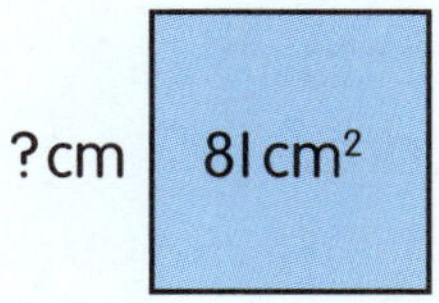

18 The area of a rectangular picture is 108 cm^2. Its width is 9 cm.

a Find its length.

b Find the perimeter of the picture.

19 The area of a square kitchen is 16 m^2.

a Find the length of a side of the kitchen.

b Find the perimeter of the kitchen.

20 The perimeter of a square garden is 24 m.

a Find the length of its side.

b Find the area of the garden.

21 The perimeter of a rectangle is 36 m. Its length is twice as long as its width.

a Find the length and width of the rectangle.

b Find the area of the rectangle.

Home Maths

Encourage your child to try to find the perimeter and area of an object at home. You could use the cover of a book or the front of a cereal box. By measuring the length and width of the object to the nearest centimetre, they should be able to calculate the perimeter and the area.

Practice Book 4B, p.91

Let's Explore!

22 Work in groups of four.
You will need a geoboard and some rubber bands.
Make as many different rectangles as possible on the geoboard.
Make sure that all the rectangles you make have the same perimeter.
Then write down your answers like this:

Example

Rectangle	Length	Width	Perimeter	Area
A	3 cm	3 cm	12 cm	9 cm^2
B	4 cm	2 cm	12 cm	8 cm^2

What do you notice about the area of these rectangles?

Let's Learn!

Composite shapes

1

A farmer wants to put a fence up around the piece of land ABCDEF.
What is the perimeter of the land?

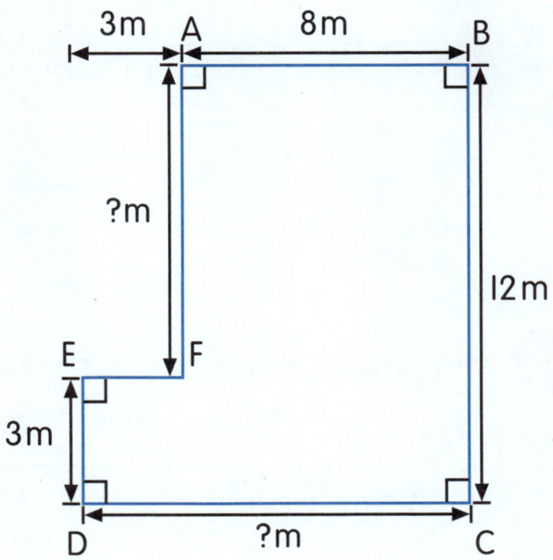

CD = EF + AB
= 3 + 8
= 11 m

AF = BC – DE
= 12 – 3
= 9 m

Perimeter of land ABCDEF = AB + BC + CD + DE + EF + AF
= 8 + 12 + 11 + 3 + 3 + 9
= 46 m

2 Find the perimeter of the shape ABCDEF.

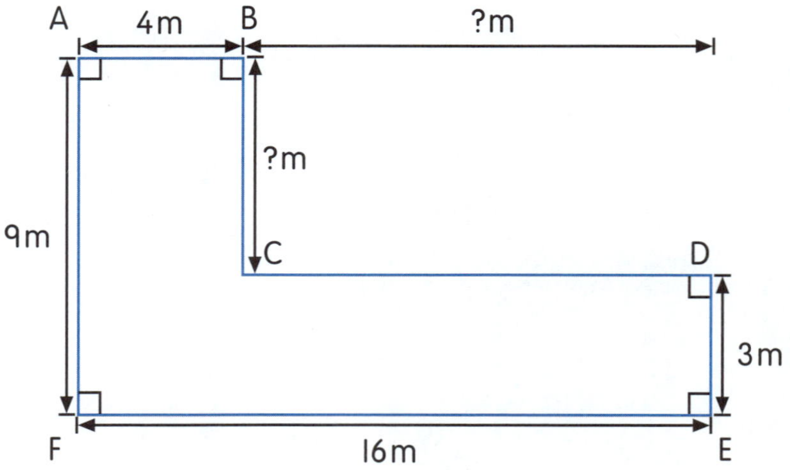

BC = AF – DE

= ___ – ___

= ___ m

CD = ___ – ___

= ___ – ___

= ___ m

Perimeter of shape ABCDEF

= ___ + ___ + ___ + ___ + ___ + ___

= ___ + ___ + ___ + ___ + ___ + ___

= ___ m

3 Find the perimeter of each shape. (All lines meet at right angles.)

a

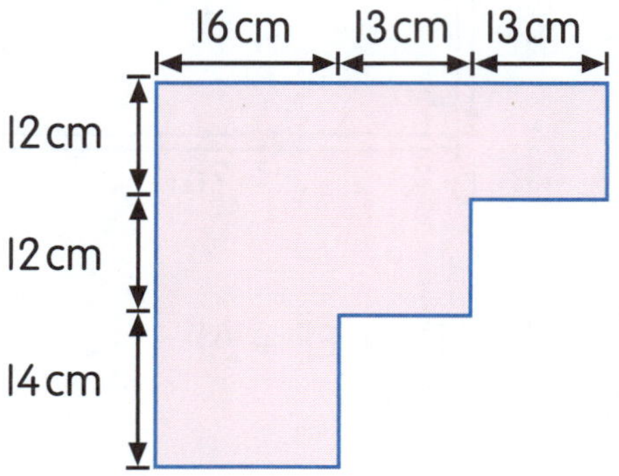

b

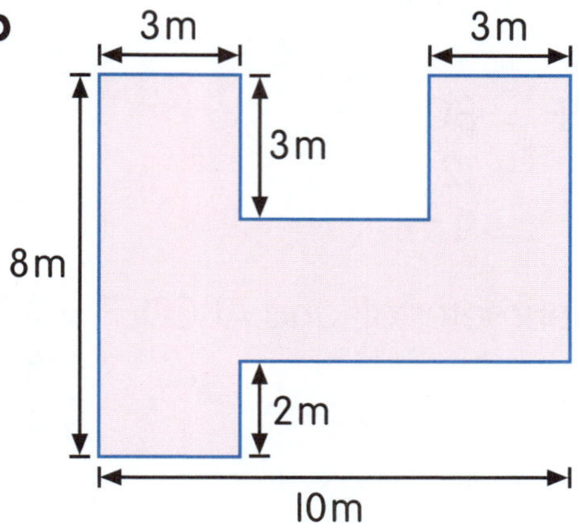

4 Find the area of the shape below.

This shape is made up of 2 or more smaller rectangles. It is called a **composite shape**.

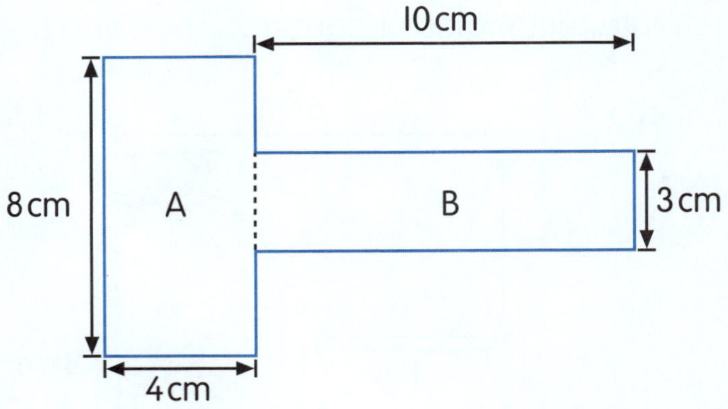

Area of Rectangle = Length × Width
Area of Rectangle A = $8 \times 4 = 32\ \text{cm}^2$
Area of Rectangle B = $10 \times 3 = 30\ \text{cm}^2$
Area of the shape = Area of Rectangle A + Area of Rectangle B
= $32 + 30$
= $62\ \text{cm}^2$

5 Find the area of the shape below.
It is made up of a square and a rectangle.

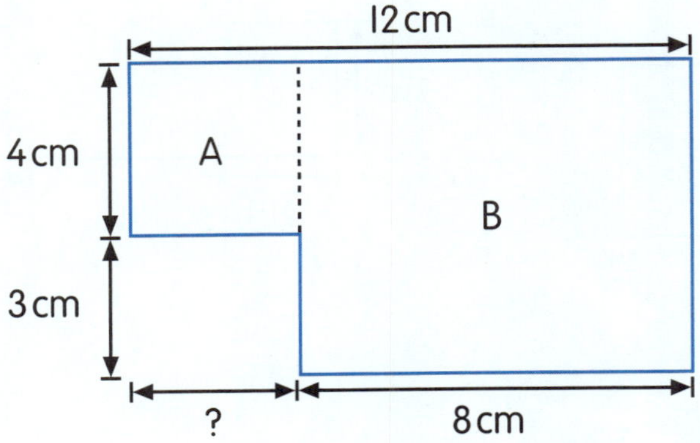

Area of Square A = ____ × ____
= ____ cm^2

Area of Rectangle B = ____ × ____
= ____ cm^2

Area of the shape = ____ + ____ = ____ cm^2

I can also divide the shape into two rectangles like this.

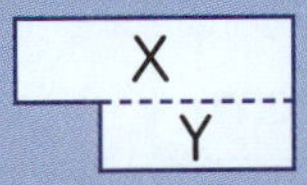

How do I find the area now?

6 Trace the shapes below. Add dotted lines to divide each shape into rectangles or squares. Then find the area of each shape.

a

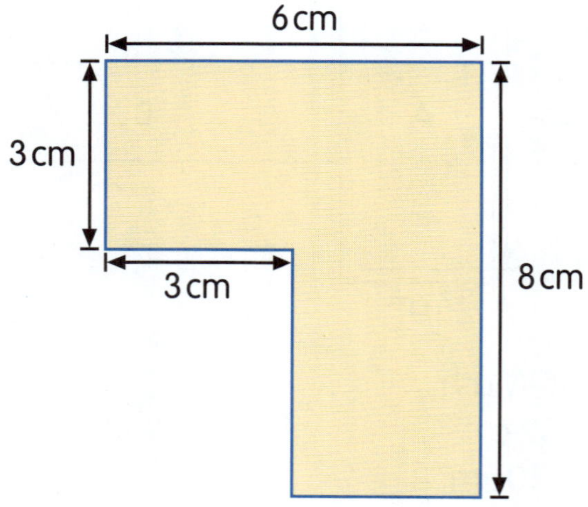

b

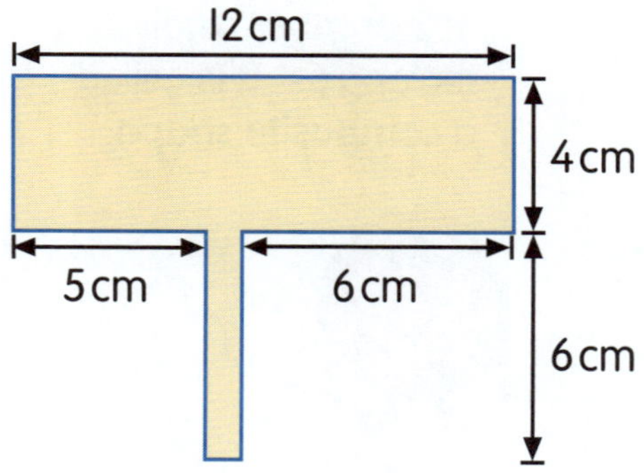

c

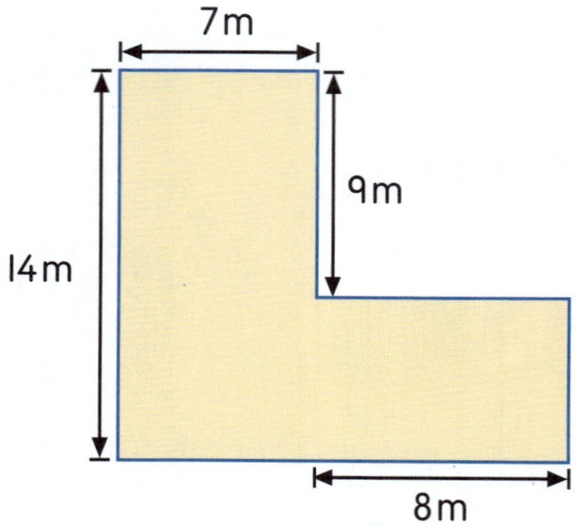

d

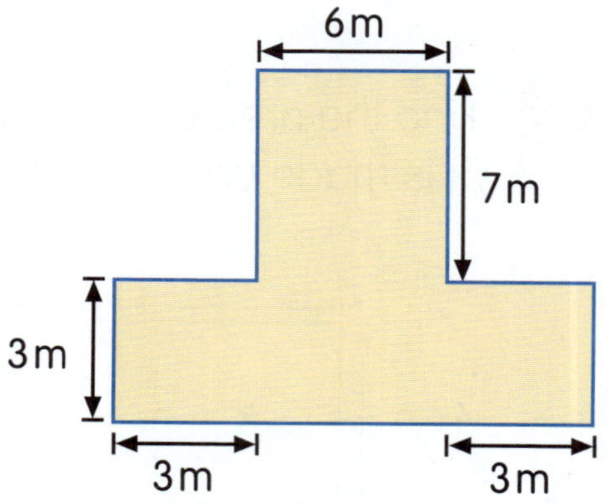

e

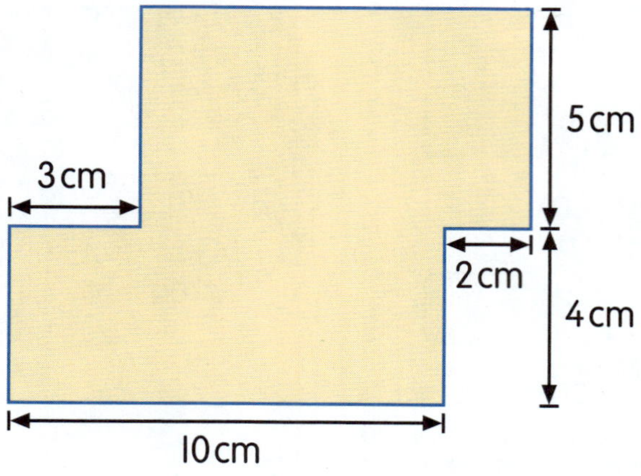

Activity

7 Work in pairs.

You will need some sheets of paper, a ruler and a pair of scissors.

1 Draw two rectangles on a sheet of paper and cut them out.

2 Draw one rectangle and one square on a sheet of paper and cut them out.

3 Draw two rectangles and one square on a sheet of paper and cut them out.

4 Make as many different shapes as you can using each set of cut-outs.

Example

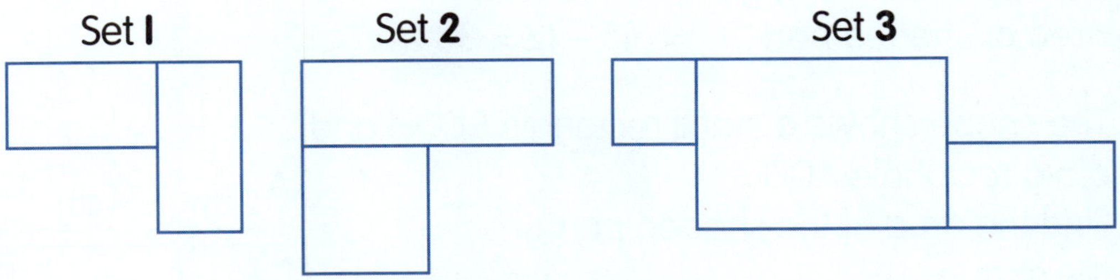

5 Then draw the shapes you made on another sheet of paper. Compare your shapes with those of your friends.

6 Alternatively, you could use a computer to draw the squares and rectangles and put them together.

Practice Book 4B, p.93

Let's Learn!

Solving word problems

1 The shape shows a small rectangle BCDG and a big rectangle ACEF. Find the area of the shaded part of the shape.

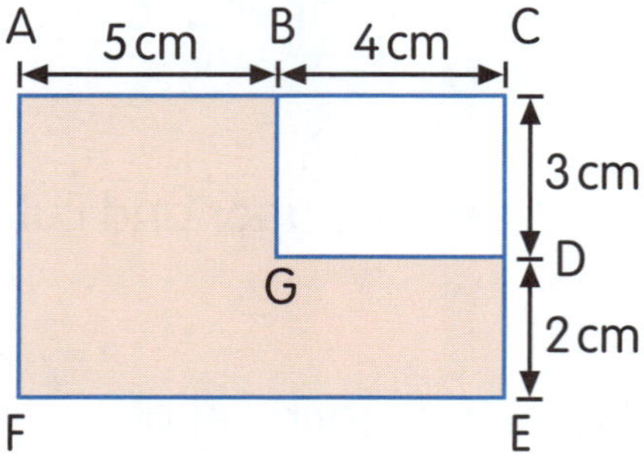

Length of big rectangle = AC = 5 + 4 = 9 cm
Width of big rectangle = CE = 3 + 2 = 5 cm
Area of big rectangle = $9 \times 5 = 45$ cm²
Area of small rectangle = $4 \times 3 = 12$ cm²
Area of shaded part = $45 - 12 = 33$ cm²

2 The shape shows a small rectangle BCGH and a big rectangle ADEF. Find the area of the shaded part of the shape.

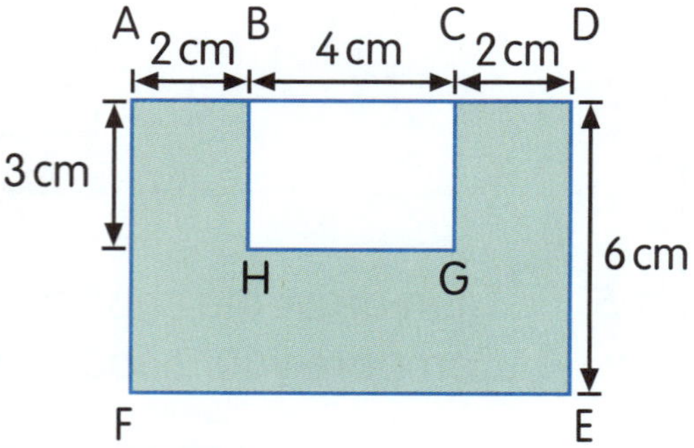

Length of big rectangle = ____ + ____ + ____
= ____ cm

Width of big rectangle = ____ cm

Area of big rectangle = ____ × ____ = ____ cm²

Area of small rectangle = ____ × ____ = ____ cm²

Area of shaded part = ____ − ____ = ____ cm²

3 The shape shows a rectangular field with a path 2 m wide around it. Find the area of the path.

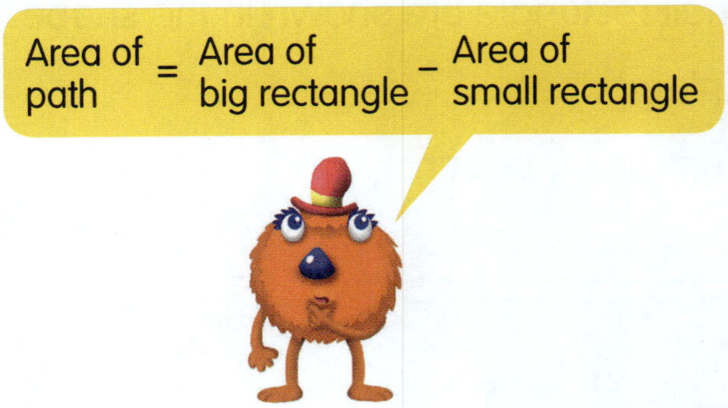

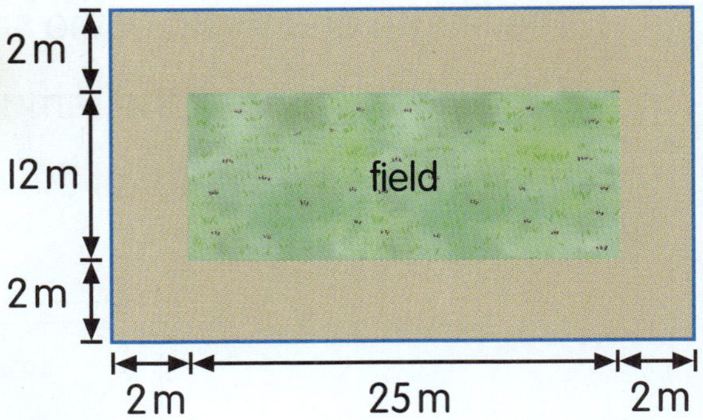

Length of big rectangle = 25 + 2 + 2 = 29 m
Width of big rectangle = 12 + 2 + 2 = 16 m
Area of big rectangle = $29 \times 16 = 464\ m^2$
Area of small rectangle = $25 \times 12 = 300\ m^2$
Area of path = $464 - 300 = 164\ m^2$

4 A rectangular piece of cloth measures 80 cm by 60 cm. When it is placed on a table, it leaves a margin 5 cm wide all around it. Find the area of the table not covered by the cloth.

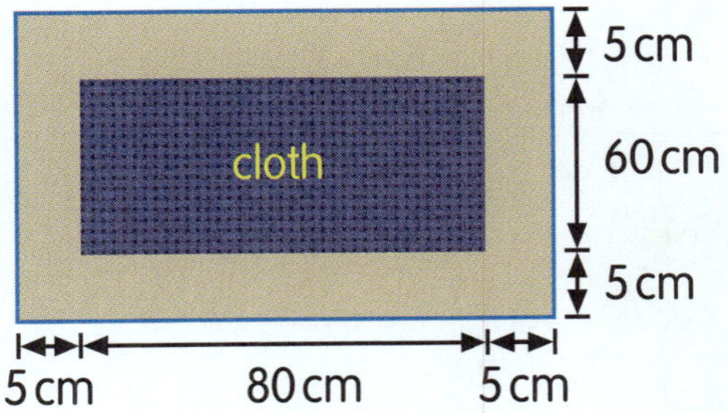

Length of table = ☐ + ☐ + ☐ = ☐ cm

Width of table = ☐ + ☐ + ☐ = ☐ cm

Area of table = ☐ × ☐ = ☐ cm^2

Area of cloth = ☐ × ☐ = ☐ cm^2

Area of table not covered by cloth = ☐ − ☐
= ☐ cm^2

5 Hardeep has a sheet of paper 13 cm long and 8 cm wide.
He cuts away a small rectangle at one of its corners.
The length and width of the small rectangle are shown in the shape.

a Find the area of the remaining paper.

b Find the perimeter of the remaining paper.

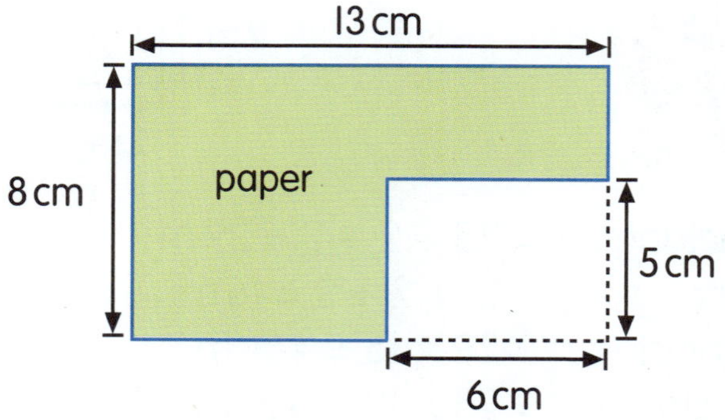

6 Sophie laid a path 1·5 m wide around a rectangular piece of land.
The length and width of the outer path are shown in the shape.

a Find the area of the rectangular land.

b Find the perimeter of the rectangular land.

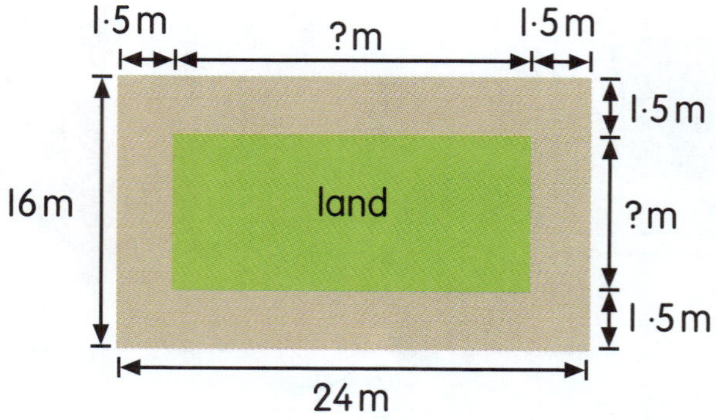

7 A corner of a square piece of paper is folded.

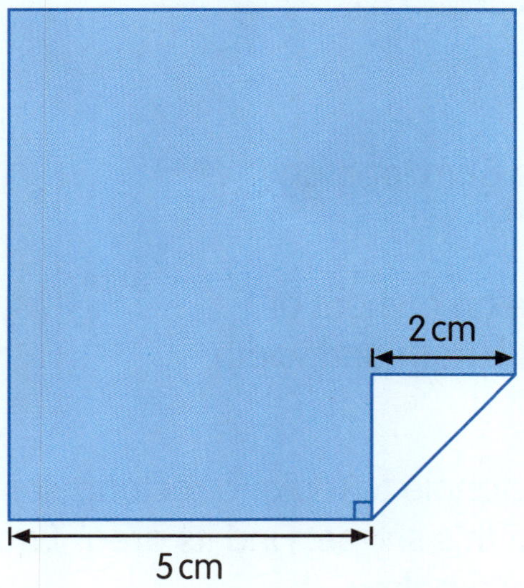

a What is the perimeter of the unfolded square piece of paper?

b What is the area of the unfolded square piece of paper?

a A side of the square = 5 + 2
= 7 cm
Perimeter of the square = 4 × 7
= 28 cm

b Area of the square = 7 × 7
= 49 cm^2

8 A rectangular piece of paper is folded at one of its corners so that the edge BC lies along the edge CD as shown.

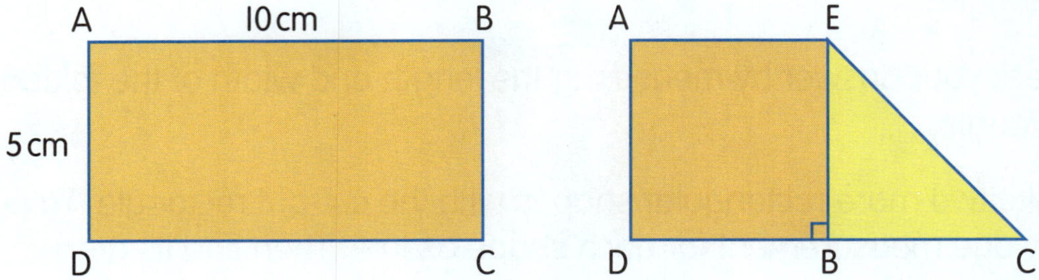

a What is the area of the rectangle before it is folded?

b What fraction of the area of the rectangle is the area of the shape AECBD?

Let's Explore!

9

1 Cut out a rectangle 8 cm long and 6 cm wide.

2 Draw this rectangle on a sheet of paper and label its length and width. Find its area.

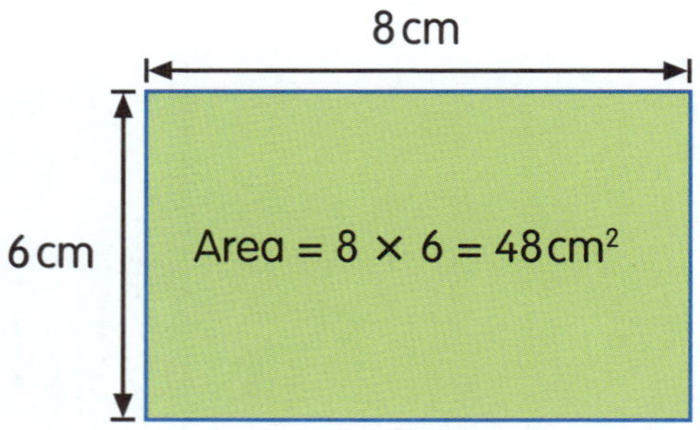

3 Fold the cut-out rectangle to make a rectangular shape. Measure the length and width of this shape. Find its area. Two examples of folded rectangles are shown below.

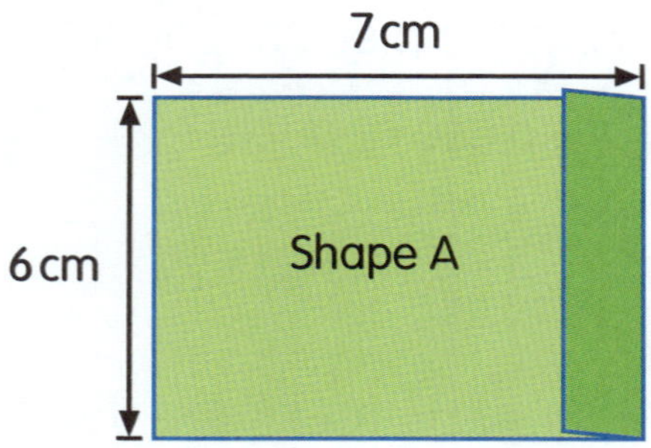

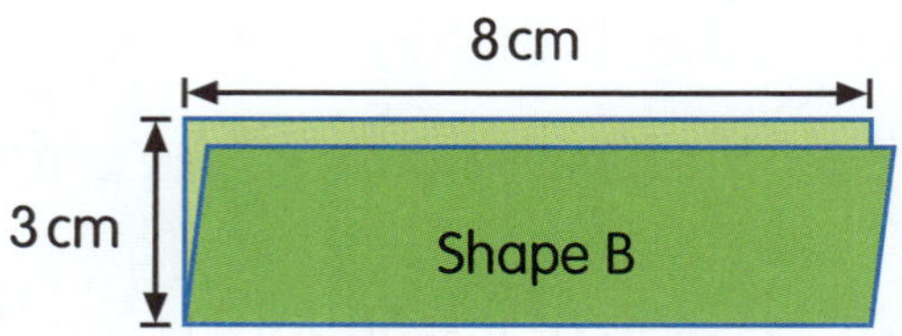

In Shape A, the length is changed by the folding. In Shape B, the width is changed by the folding.

4 Unfold the rectangle you made in **3**. Fold it to make another rectangular shape. This time take only one measurement – measure the side that is changed by the folding. Then find the area of the folded rectangle.

5 Check your answer by measuring the length and width of the folded rectangle.

6 Make two more rectangular shapes with the cut-out rectangle. Take only one measurement for each shape as in **4**. Then find its area.

7 Does your method of using one measurement to find the area apply for these shapes too?

Practice Book 4B, p.97

Maths Journal

10 The list below shows what has been covered in this unit. Write down which parts of this unit you like the most and which parts you find difficult.

Area and Perimeter

a Find the length of one side of a rectangle given its perimeter and the other side.

b Find the length of the sides of a square given its perimeter.

c Find the length of one side of a rectangle given its area and the other side.

d Find the length of the sides of a square given its area.

e Find the perimeter of a composite shape.

f Find the area of a composite shape by dividing the shape into different types of rectangles.

Put On Your Thinking Caps!

11 **a** What is the length of the side of a square if its perimeter and area have the same numerical value?
(Hint: Make a systematic list.)

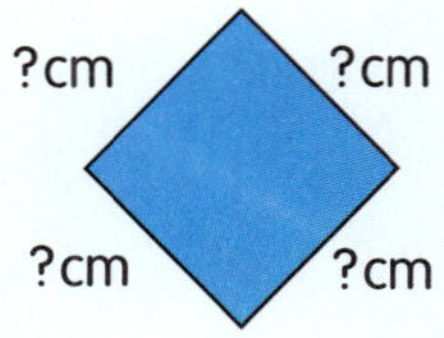

b Ella has a rectangular piece of paper 12 cm long and 8 cm wide. How many squares can she draw on the piece of paper, without overlapping, if the side of each square is 3 cm long?

c Look at the shape. All sides of the shape meet at right angles.
What is the perimeter of the shape?

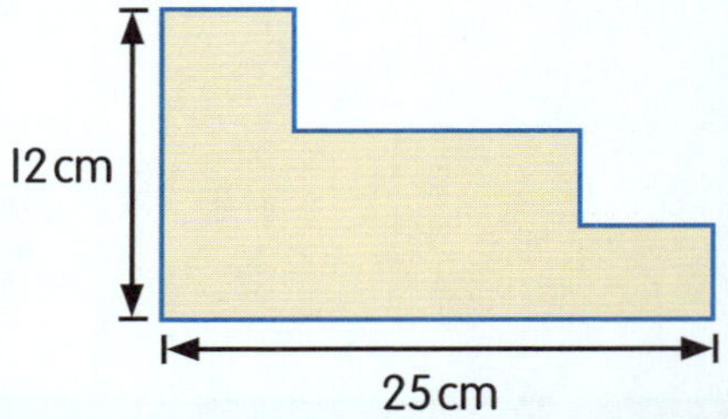

Put On Your Thinking Caps!

d Jack arranged two different square pieces of paper as shown. The length of the side of each square piece of paper is a whole number.

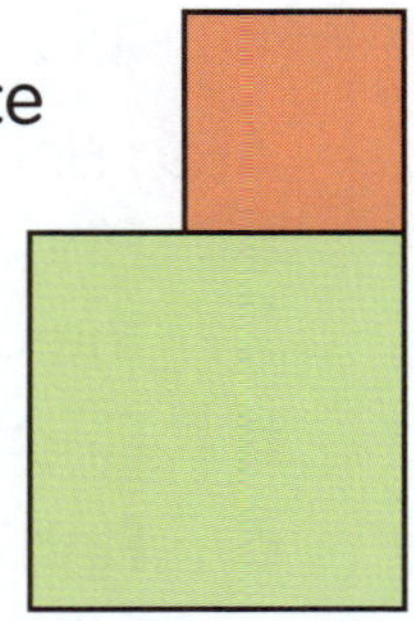

The total area of the shape is 89 cm^2. What is the length of the side of each square piece of paper? Copy the table below and complete it to find out the answer.

Length of the Square (cm)	1	2	3	4	5	6	7	8	9	10
Area of the Square (cm^2)	1	4	9							

Practice Book 4B, p.101

Practice Book 4B, p.103

Unit 13 Symmetry

Let's Learn!

Identifying symmetrical shapes

1 These are symmetrical shapes.

The dotted line in each shape is a **line of symmetry**.

2 Fold shape A along the **line of symmetry**.

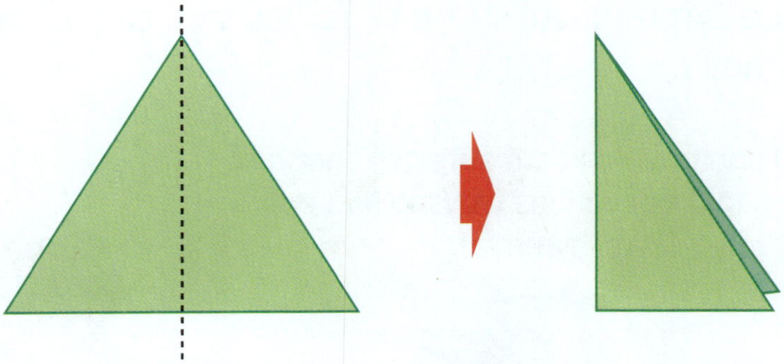

The shape is divided into equal halves by the **line of symmetry**.
The two equal halves fit exactly. So Shape A is a symmetrical shape.

3 Fold Shape B along the dotted line as shown.

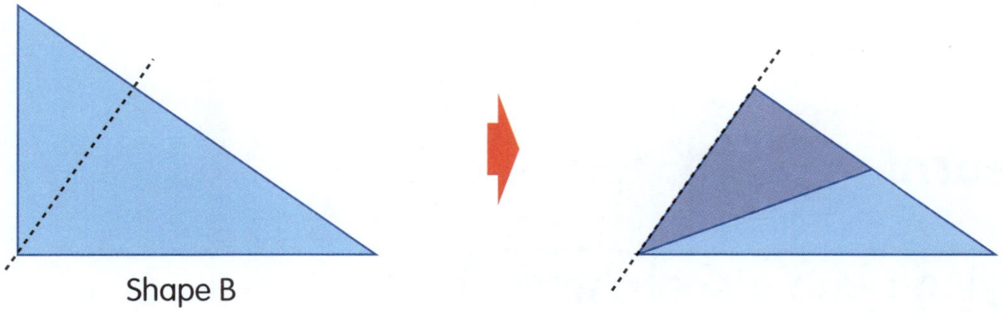

Shape B

The two parts do not fit exactly. The dotted line is **not** a line of symmetry. We cannot find a line of symmetry on this shape. Shape B is not a symmetrical shape.

How do we recognise a symmetrical shape?

A symmetrical shape has a line of symmetry. This line divides the shape into two equal halves. When folded along the line of symmetry, the halves fit exactly.

4 Which of the following are symmetrical shapes? To find out, check if each shape has a line of symmetry.

You can trace and cut out each shape. Then fold it in various ways to find out if it has a line of symmetry.

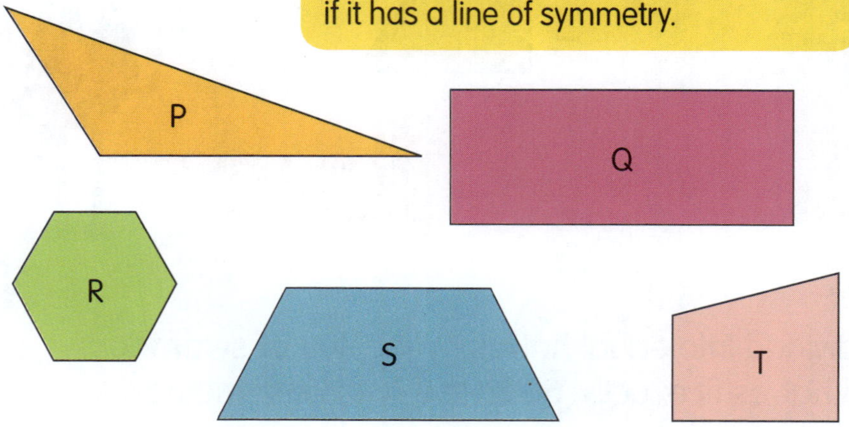

5 The letters P and Q are not symmetrical shapes.

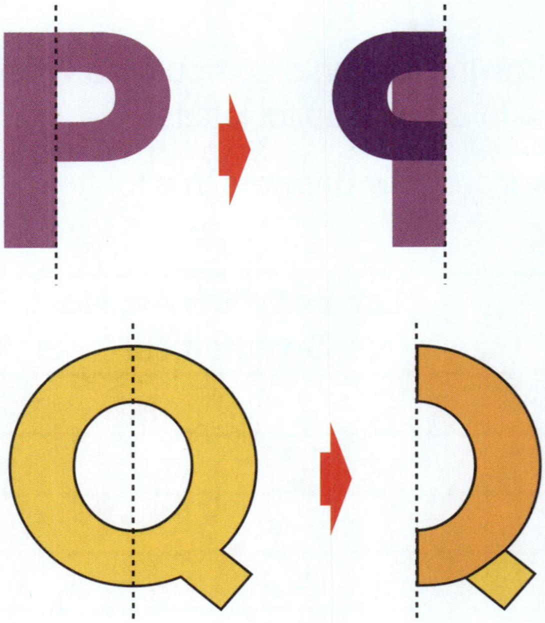

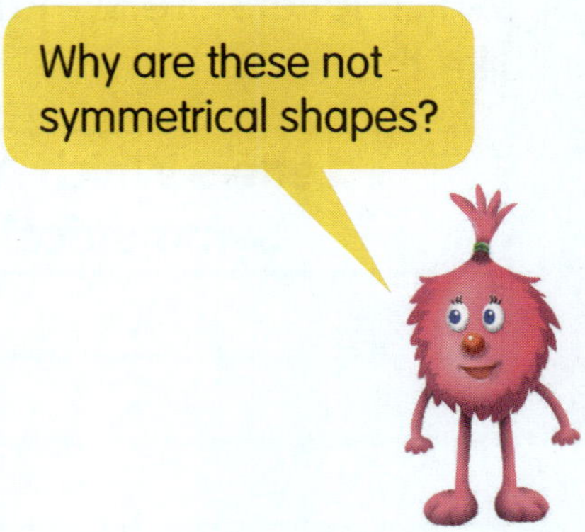

6 Which of these are **not** symmetrical shapes?

Shapes [ ] are not symmetrical shapes.

Home Maths

Ask your child to trace and cut out the shapes in **6**.
Then fold the shapes along the dotted lines.
Ask them to show you which shapes are symmetrical and explain why.

Activity

7 Use a pencil and paper or the drawing tool on a computer to write the letters of the alphabet from A to Z. Use capital letters.

Which letters are symmetrical? Record your answers in a table like this:

Letters Which Are Symmetrical	Letters Which Are Not Symmetrical
X	R

8 Which of these shapes are symmetrical?

a

b

c

d

9 Which of the pictures below are symmetrical?

Can you find more symmetrical shapes and objects around you?

10 Which of these are symmetrical shapes?

a

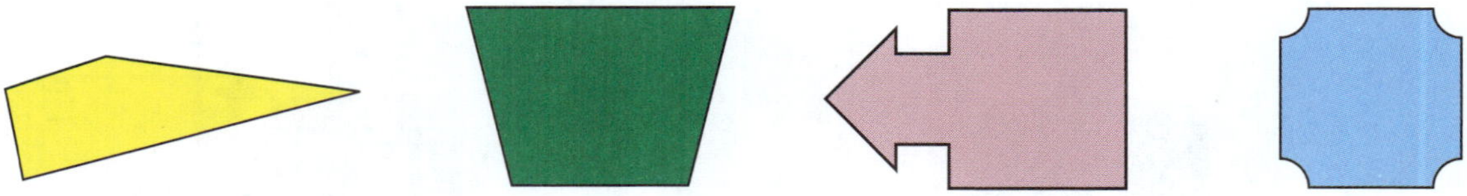

A B C D

b

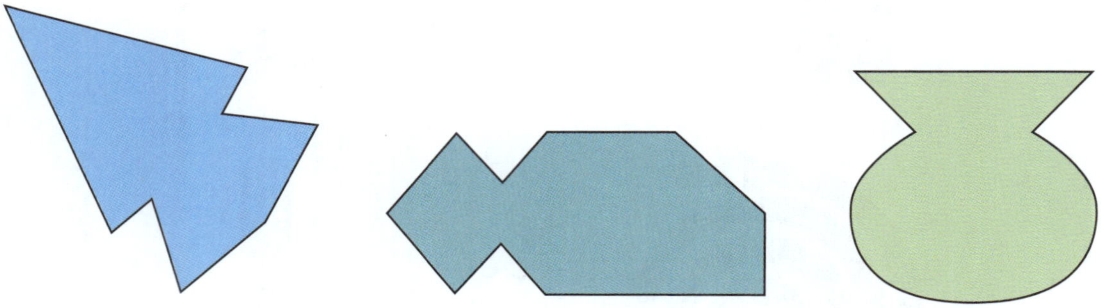

E F G

11 Ella drew the picture below using her computer. How many symmetrical shapes can you find in her picture?

Practice Book 4B, p.109

Let's Learn!

Identifying lines of symmetry

1. Fold Shape A along the dotted line as shown.

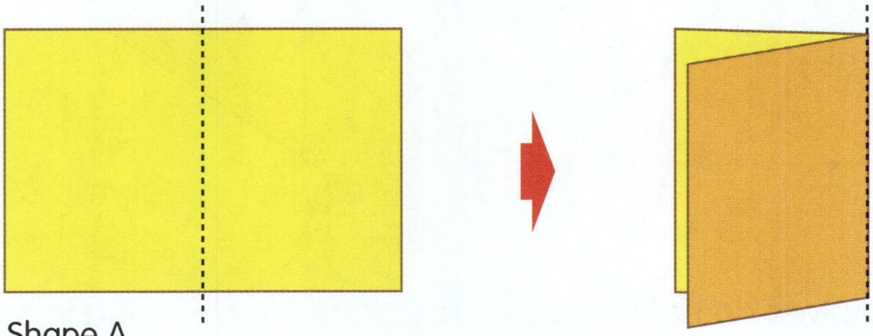

Shape A

The two parts fit exactly. They are equal halves. The dotted line is a line of symmetry of Shape A.

2. Now fold Shape A along the dotted line as shown.

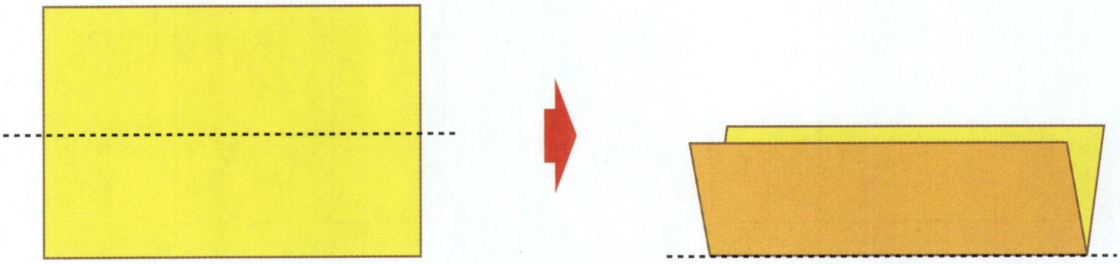

Shape A

The two parts fit exactly. They are equal halves. The dotted line is another line of symmetry of Shape A.

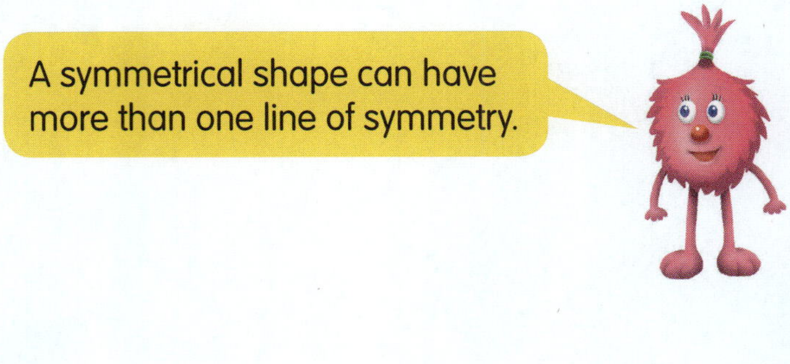

3 Look at the two halves made by the dotted line. Do the two halves fit exactly? Is the dotted line a line of symmetry of Shape A?

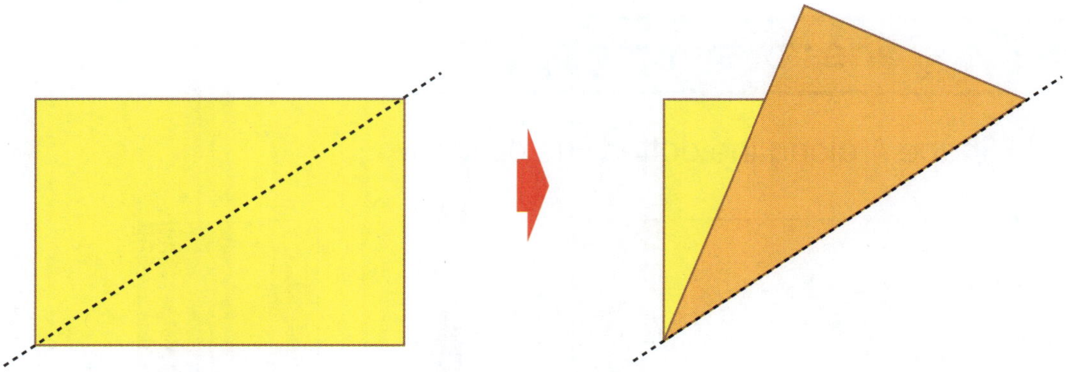

Shape A

The two halves do not fit exactly. The dotted line is **not** a line of symmetry of Shape A.

4 Is the dotted line a line of symmetry of Shape A?

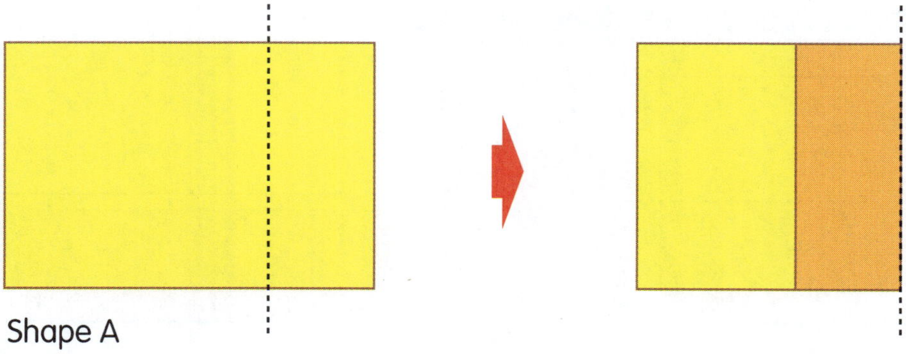

Shape A

The two parts do not fit exactly. The two parts are not equal.

The dotted line is ______.

5 Look at the following diagrams of Shape X. In each diagram, the dotted line divides Shape X into two equal parts. Trace the four diagrams of Shape X and cut them out.

Which of the dotted lines are lines of symmetry of Shape X?

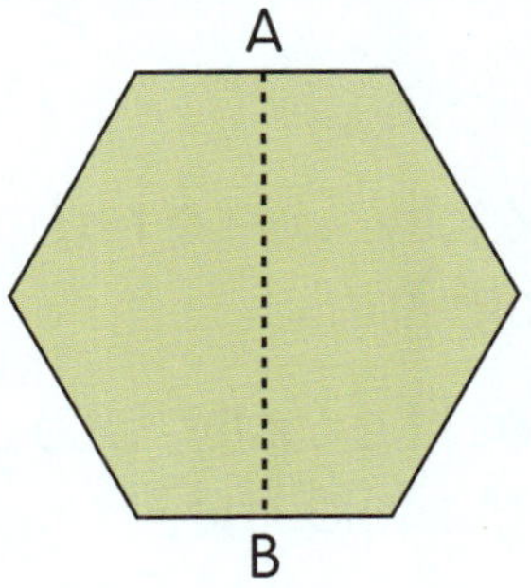

Shape X

Fold Shape X along the line AB.

The two parts ____ exactly.

Line AB is ____.

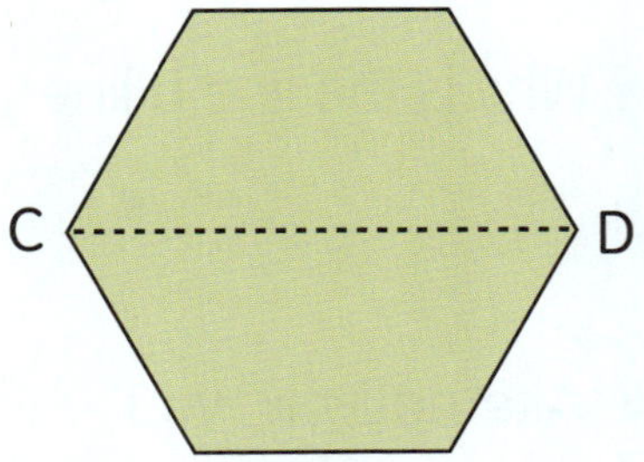

Shape X

Fold Shape X along the line CD.

The two parts ____ exactly.

Line CD is ____.

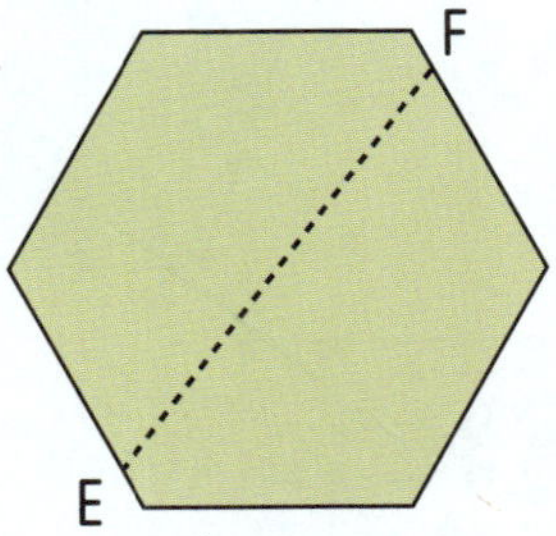

Shape X

Fold Shape X along the line EF.

The two parts ____ exactly.

Line EF is ____.

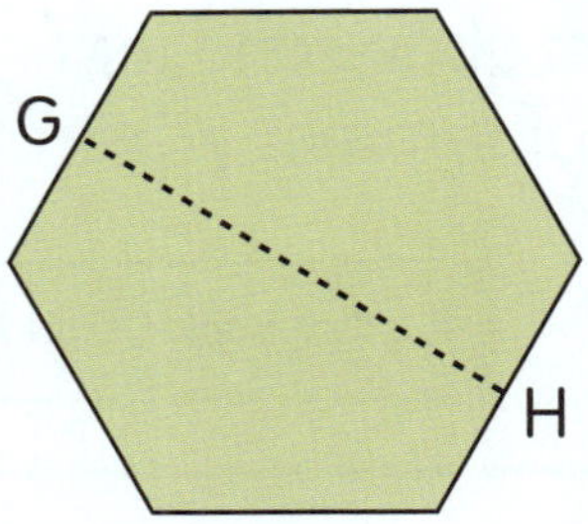

Shape X

Fold Shape X along the line GH.

The two parts ____ exactly.

Line GH is ____.

Activity

6 **a** You will need a piece of paper containing the shape on the right.

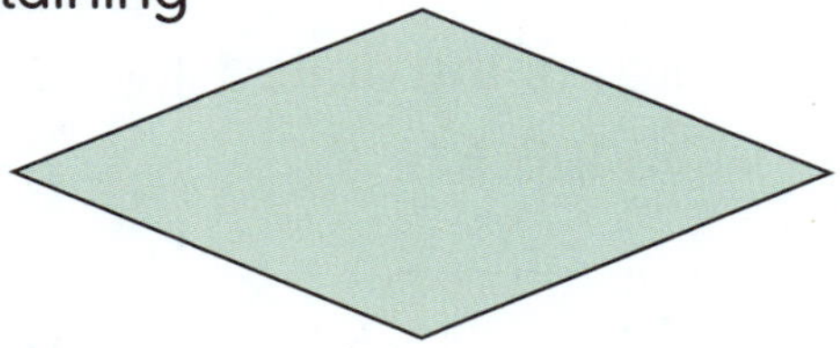

1 Cut out the shape.

2 Fold the shape to get:

i two parts which are equal and fit exactly. Use a red coloured pencil to draw along the fold line.

ii two parts which are equal but do **not** fit exactly. Use a blue coloured pencil to draw along the fold line.

iii two parts which are **not** equal and do **not** fit exactly. Use a yellow coloured pencil to draw along the fold line.

Which of these lines is a line of symmetry? Why is the line a line of symmetry?

b Trace the shapes below and cut them out. Alternatively, you could use a computer to make the shapes.

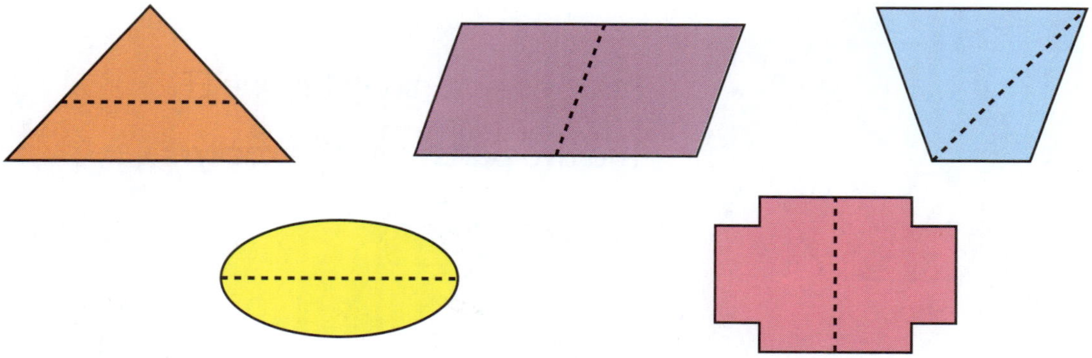

Draw a dotted line on each shape as shown above and fold along it. Which of the dotted lines are lines of symmetry?

Practice Book 4B, p.111

Let's Learn!

Making symmetrical shapes and patterns

1 **a** Jack folds a piece of paper in half. He cuts out a shape which starts and ends on the fold line like this:

Jack unfolds the shape. He gets a symmetrical shape like this:

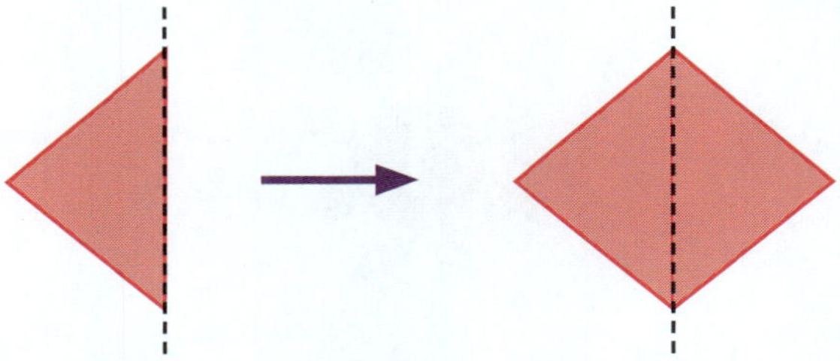

The fold line is a line of symmetry.

b Jack folds another piece of paper in half. Using the same method as before, he cuts out another symmetrical shape.

This fold line is also a line of symmetry.

2 Fold a piece of paper in half. Cut out a shape which starts from a point on the fold line and ends on another point along the same fold line. Unfold your symmetrical shape. Compare your shape with those of your friends.

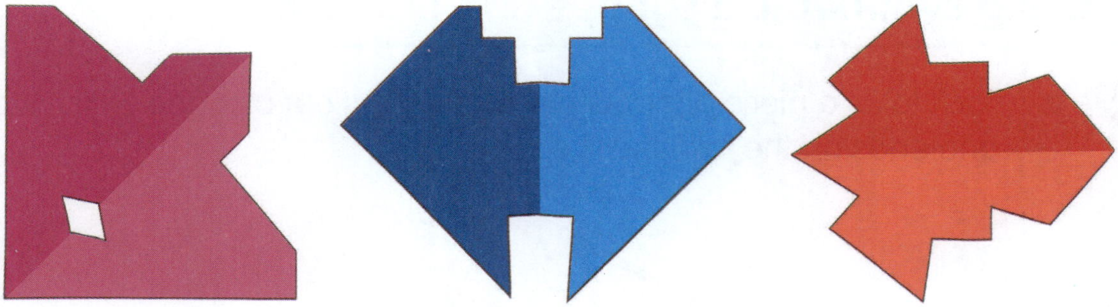

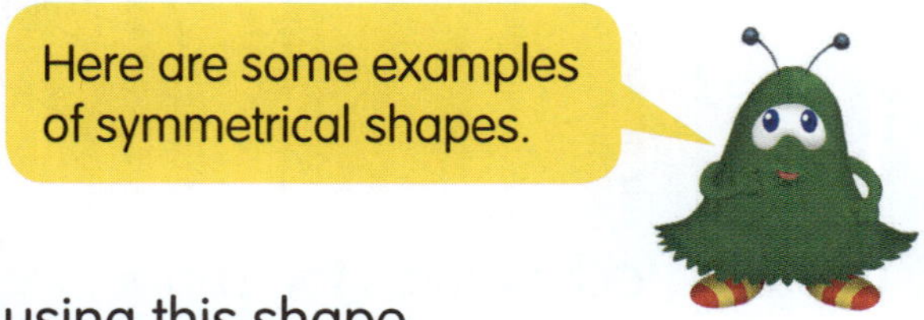

3 Tai makes a wrapping paper pattern using this shape.

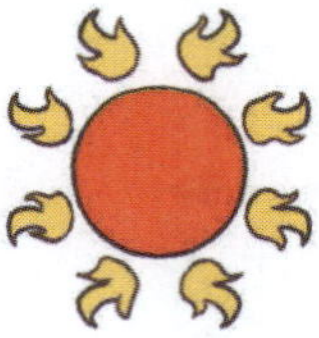

Can you find a line of symmetry in the shape?

Using this shape, he makes the pattern below on his paper.

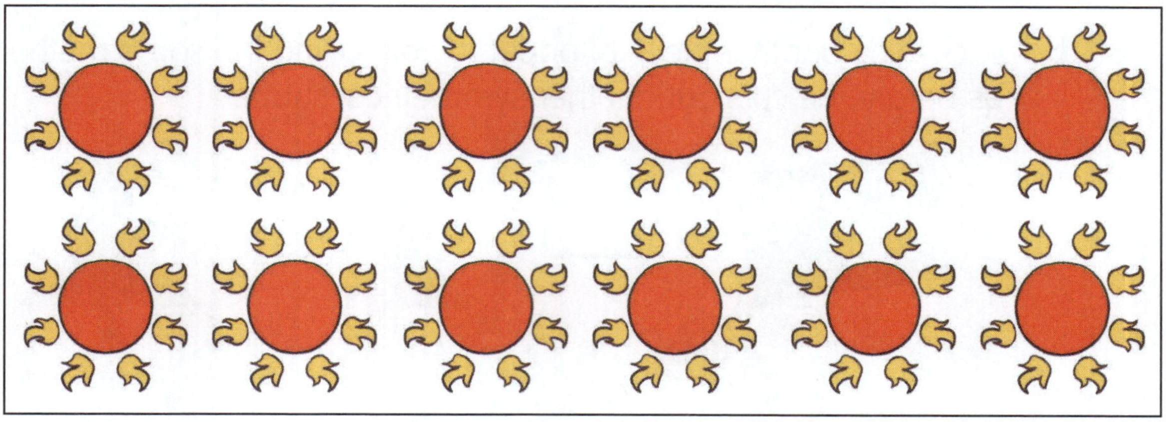

Home Maths

Visit an art gallery or clothes shop with your child. Look for pictures or clothes that have symmetrical shapes or patterns.
(1) Ask your child to draw a pattern that shows symmetrical shapes.
(2) Ask your child to draw a pattern that shows no symmetrical shapes.

Activity

4 **a** You will need some coloured paper and a big sheet of paper.

1. Fold a piece of coloured paper. Cut out a symmetrical shape.
2. Make four copies of this shape.
3. Stick the shapes on a big sheet of paper to make a pattern. Show your pattern to your teacher.

Example

b Which of these designs are made up of symmetrical shapes? What are the symmetrical shapes used in these designs?

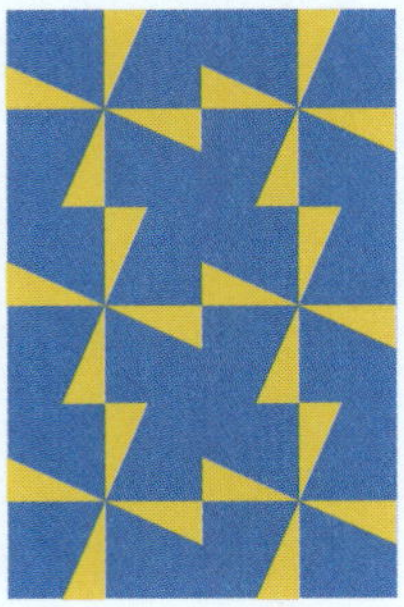

5 Each shape below is half of a symmetrical shape. Copy them onto square grid paper. Then complete each symmetrical shape using the dotted line as a line of symmetry.

a

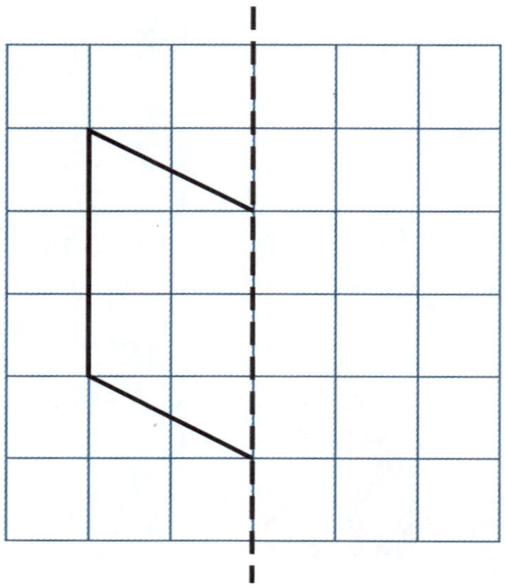

b

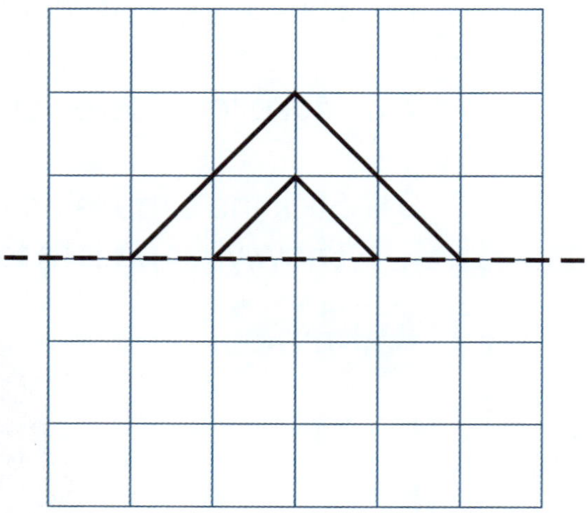

c

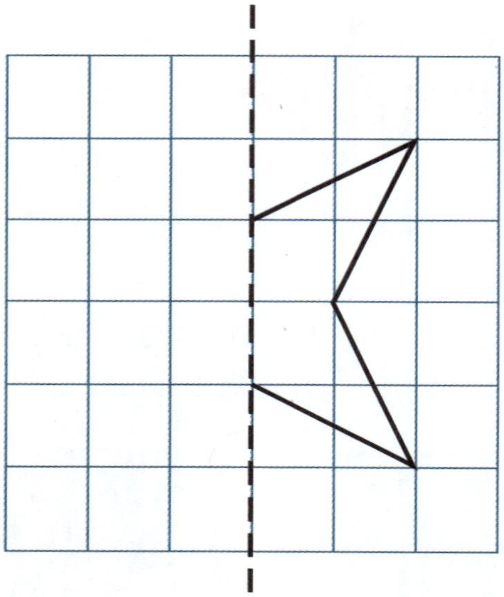

d

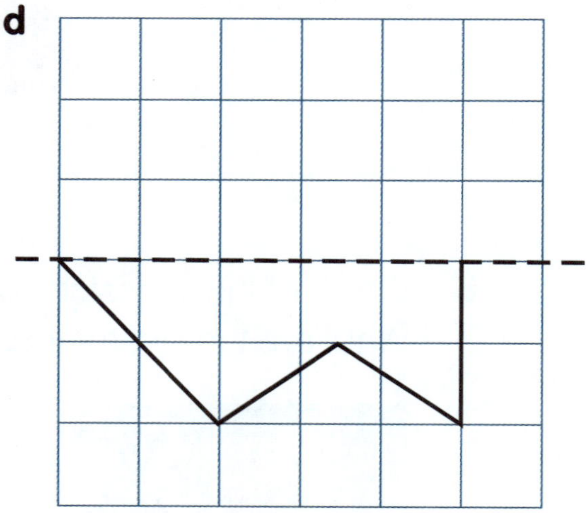

6 Omar took two rectangular pieces of square grid paper as shown below. He coloured some squares on one half of each piece of paper. Copy the rectangles and colour the squares on the other half of each piece of paper to make a symmetrical pattern.

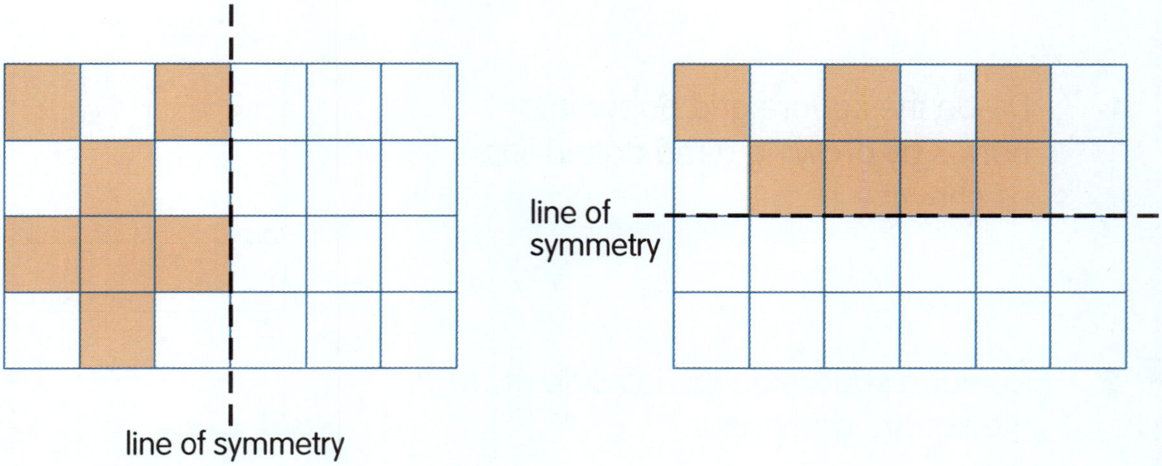

7 Each diagram below shows half of a symmetrical pattern. Copy these patterns onto square grid paper. Then complete each symmetrical pattern with the dotted line as a line of symmetry.

a

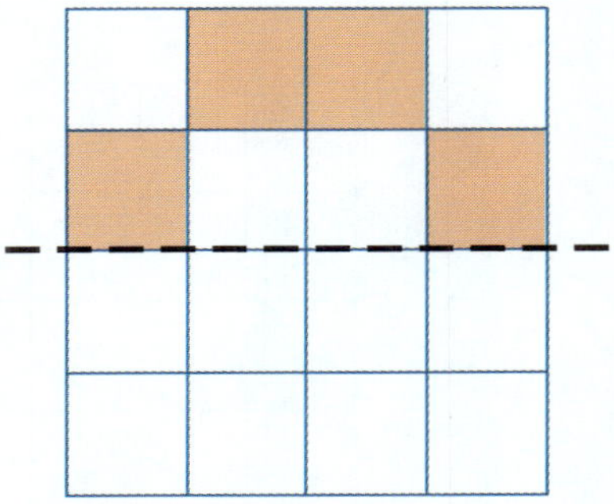

b

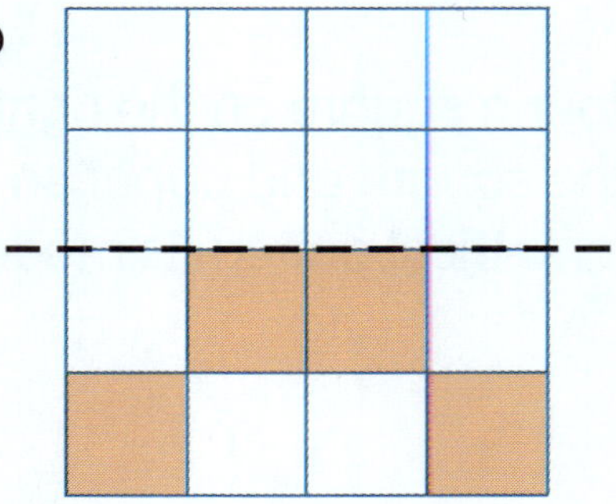

c

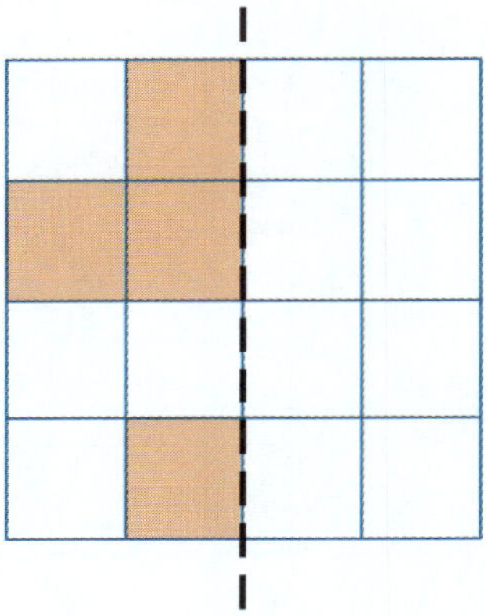

d

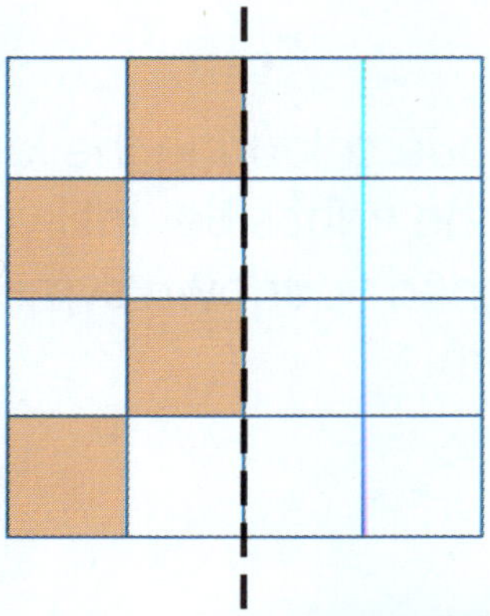

Practice Book 4B, p.113

Let's Explore!

8 You can create your own symmetrical pattern by using square grid paper and a coloured pencil.

1 Divide the square grid paper into halves by drawing a red dotted line as shown.

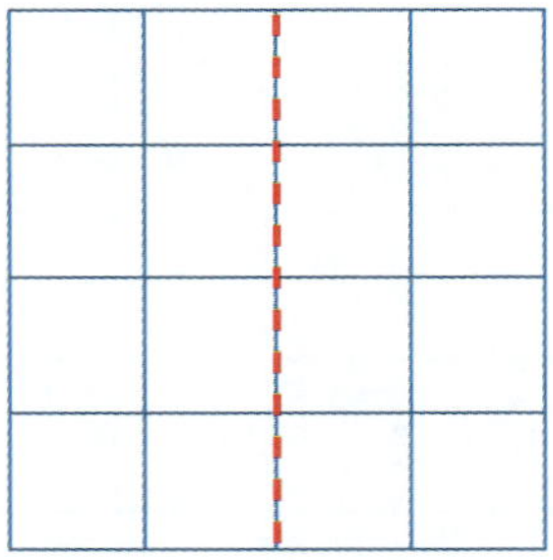

2 Colour a square on the left side of the square grid paper.

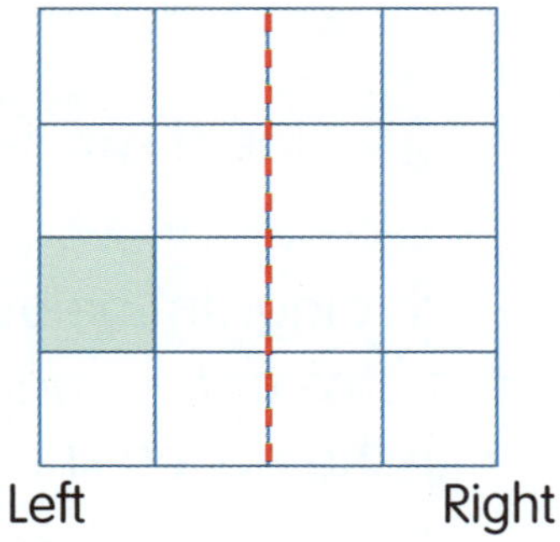

3 Colour a square on the right side of the square grid paper so that a symmetrical pattern is made.

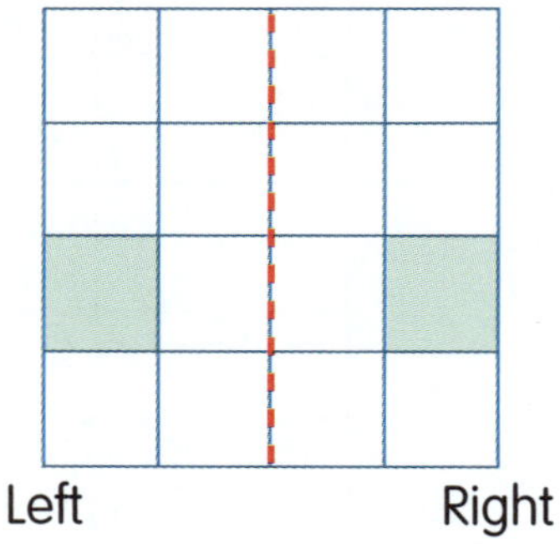

4 Continue colouring the left side, and then the right side until you have designed your own symmetrical pattern.

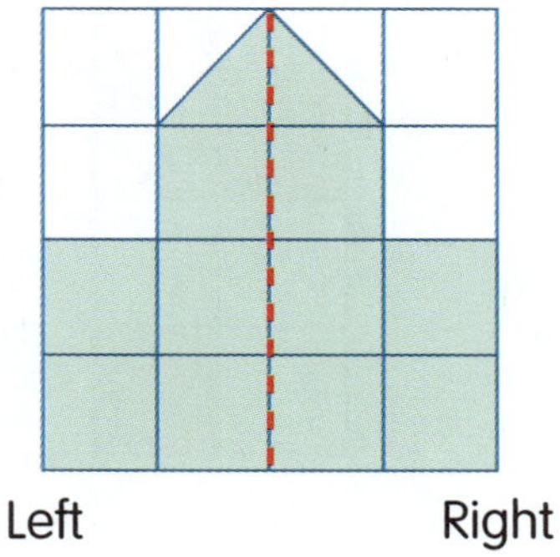

Put On Your Thinking Caps!

9 **a** Which of these patterns are symmetrical?

i

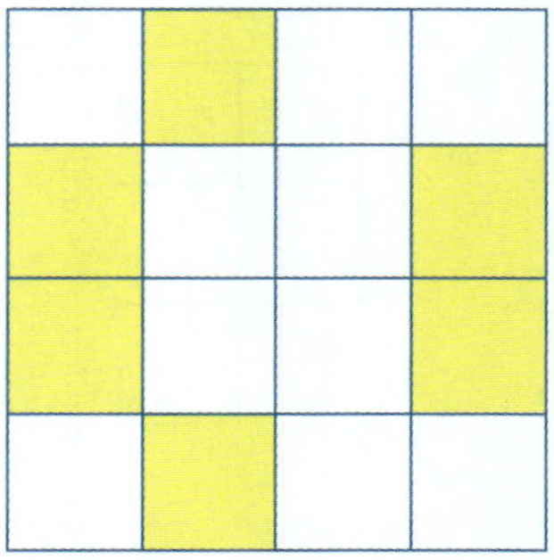

ii

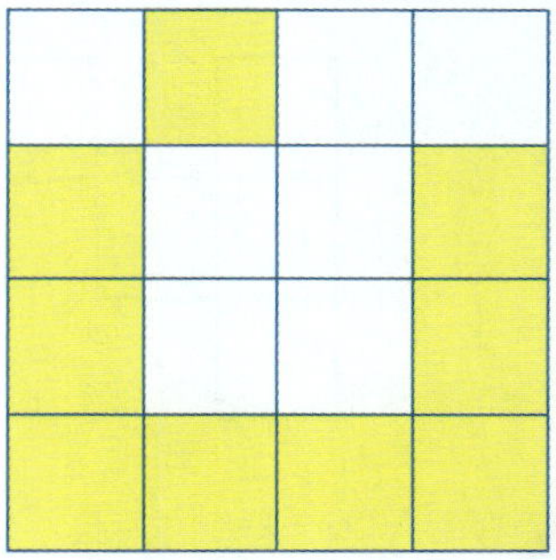

iii

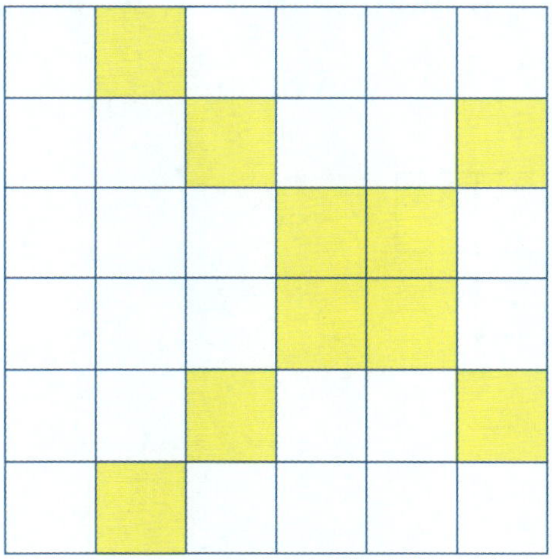

b Which pattern is not symmetrical?
On a sheet of square grid paper, copy the pattern and colour one or more squares to make it symmetrical.

Put On Your Thinking Caps!

10 On a sheet of paper, copy the patterns below and add one unit square to each pattern to make it symmetrical.

a

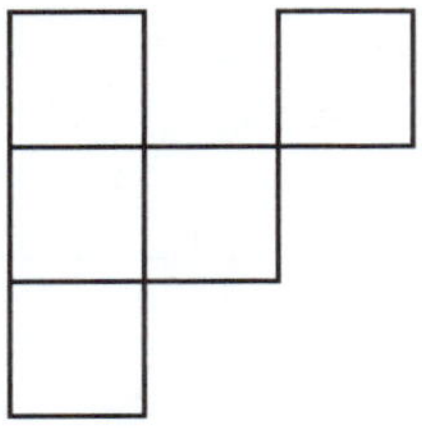

b

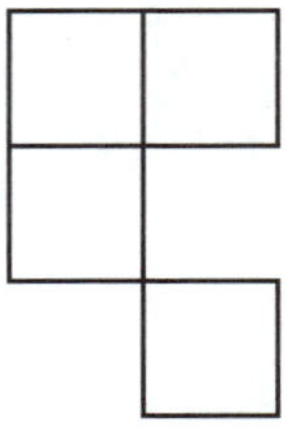

11 On a sheet of paper, copy the patterns below and add three unit squares to each pattern to make it symmetrical.

a

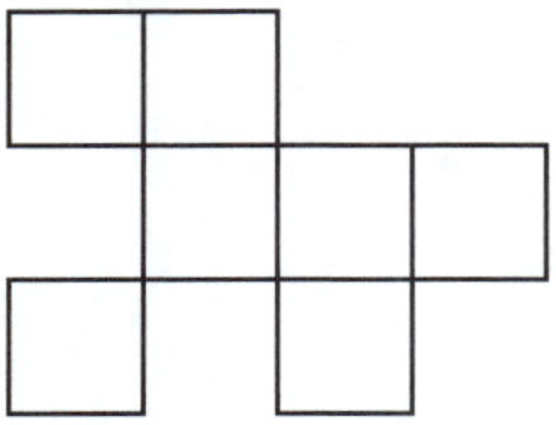

b

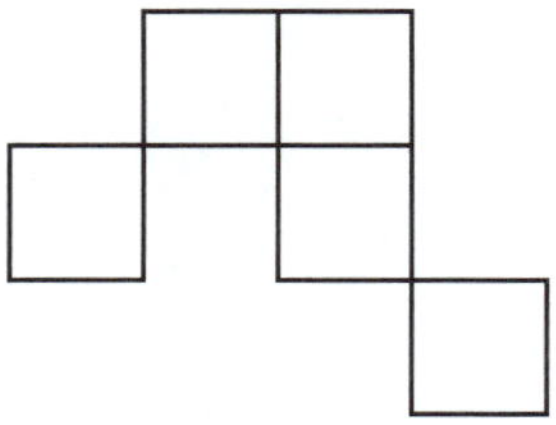

Practice Book 4B, p.117

Practice Book 4B, p.118

Unit 14 Tessellations

Let's Learn!

Identifying tessellations

1 Look at the picture below. It shows part of a floor covered with rectangular tiles.

Look at these tiles.

Tiles of each shape can be used to cover a surface with no gaps between them.

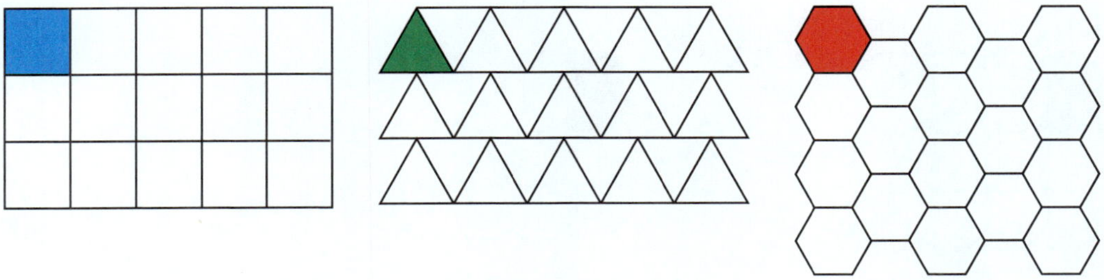

These tilling patterns are called **tessellations**. Each tessellation is made with **one** shape. This is the **unit shape** of the tessellation.

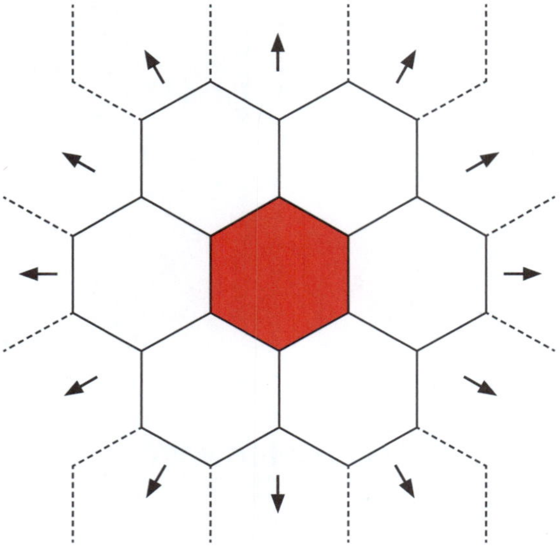

We can use the unit shape of the tessellation to build the pattern in all directions.

2 Some shapes do not tessellate.
Look at these shapes.

Shapes do not tessellate when there are gaps in between them or when they overlap.

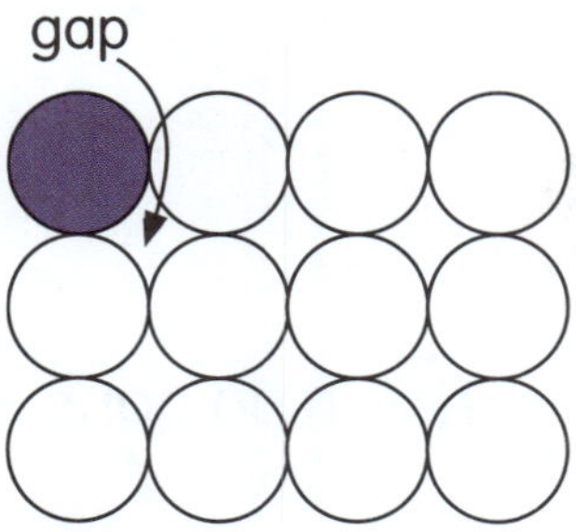

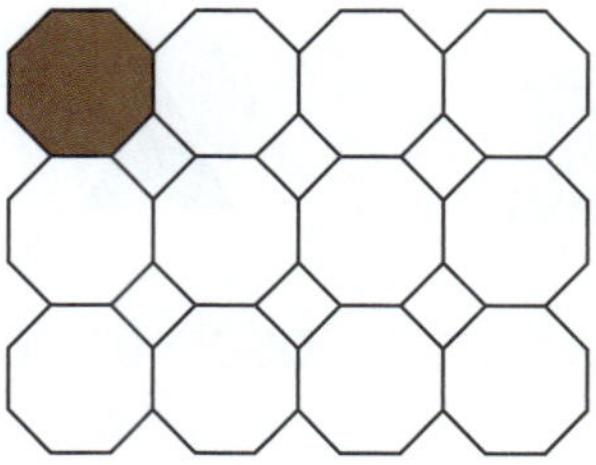

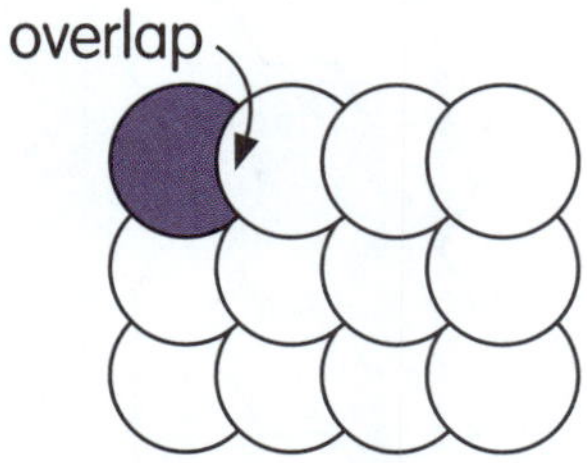

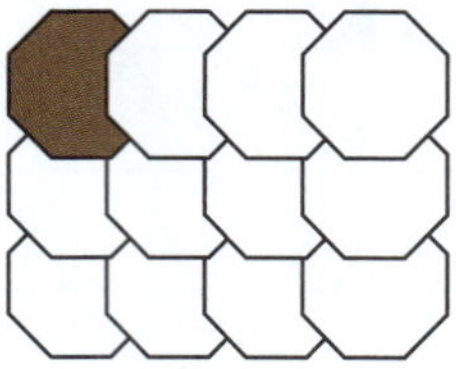

3 Identify and draw the unit shape used in each of the following tessellations.

a

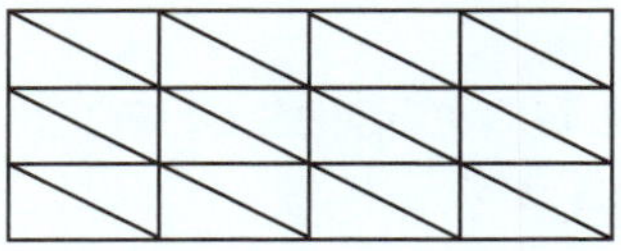

b

c

d

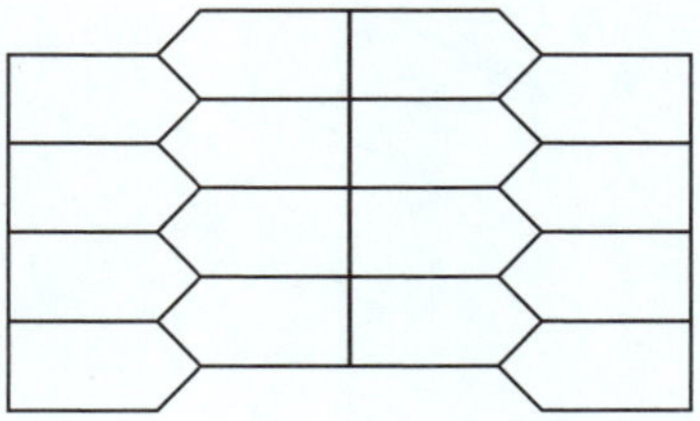

Activity

4 **a** Your teacher will give you ten copies of each of the following shapes. Find out which shapes tessellate.

1

2

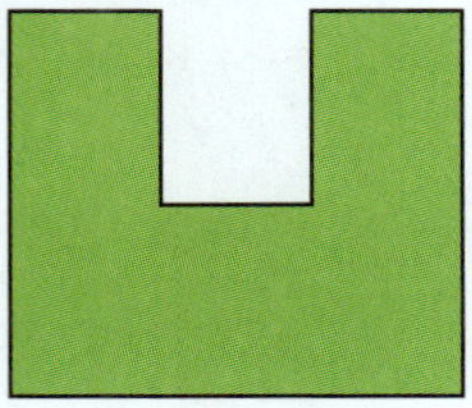

3

b Copy each of the following shapes on a piece of square dotty paper. Make a tessellation with each shape.

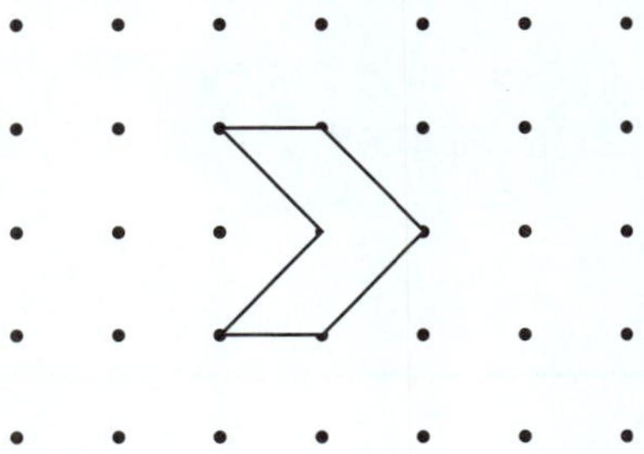

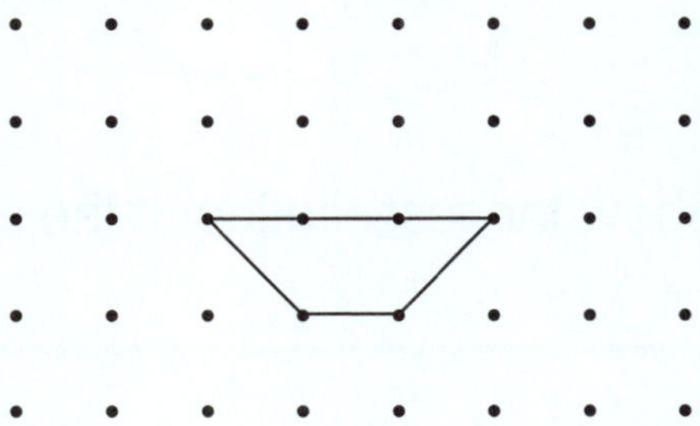

Activity

c Draw and cut out the shapes below. Make ten copies of each shape and find out which shapes tessellate.

1

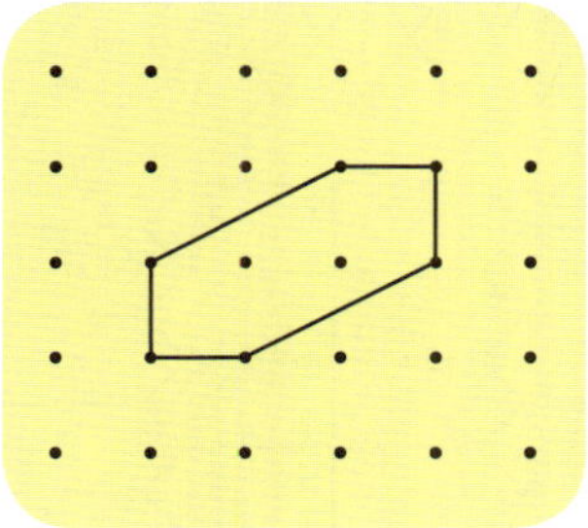

2

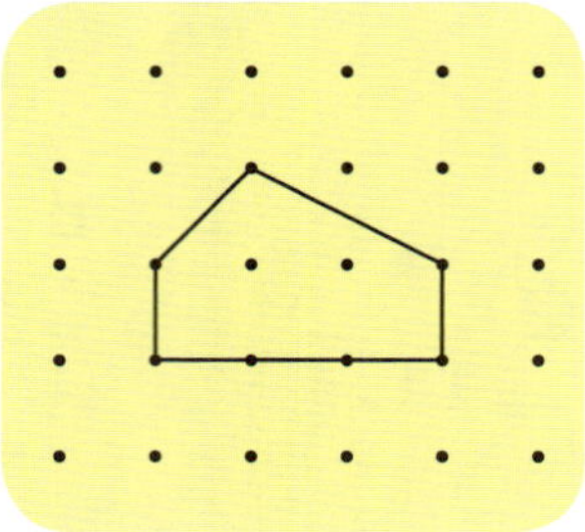

3

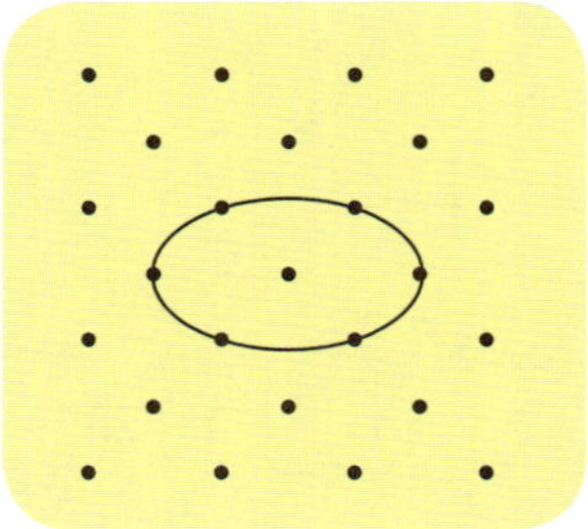

Practice Book 4B, p.119

Let's Explore!

5 Work in pairs.

1 Use a pencil, a ruler and paper or the drawing tool on a computer to draw a triangle and make twelve copies of it.

2 Cut the triangles out. Mark the angles as shown below and tessellate the triangles. Your triangle can be different from the one shown below.

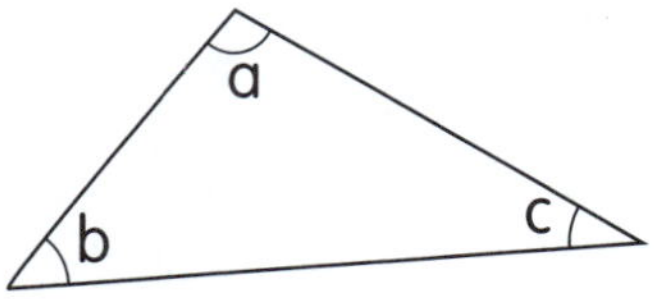

3 Show the tessellation of the triangle.

Let's Learn!

More tessellations

1 Some shapes can tessellate in more than one way.
For this shape , here are some ways it tessellates.

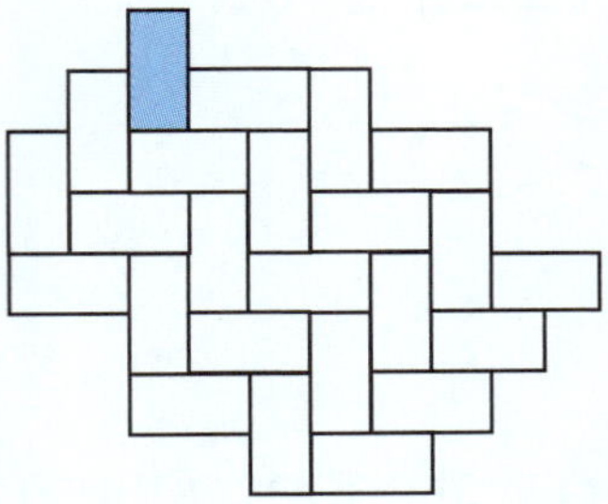

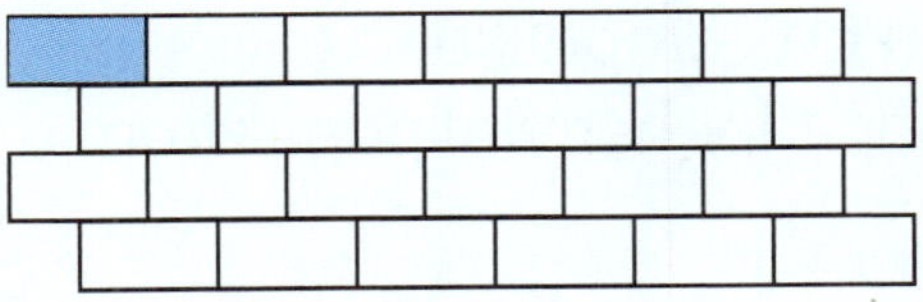

Draw another tessellation of this shape on a piece of paper.

Activity

2 Make ten copies of each shape shown below. Cut out each shape.
Tessellate it in two different ways.

a

b

c

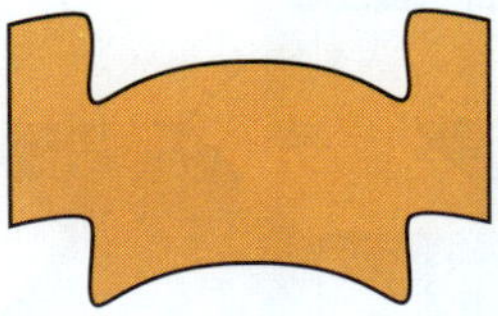

d

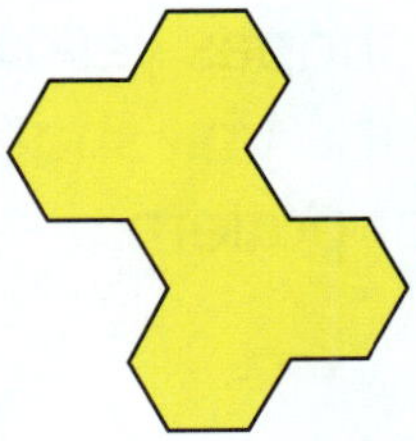

3 Draw and cut out the shapes below. Make ten copies of each shape and use them to make as many different tessellations as you can for each shape.

a

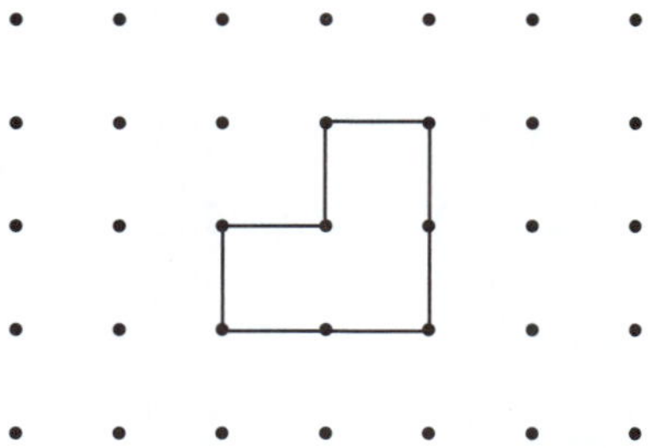

b

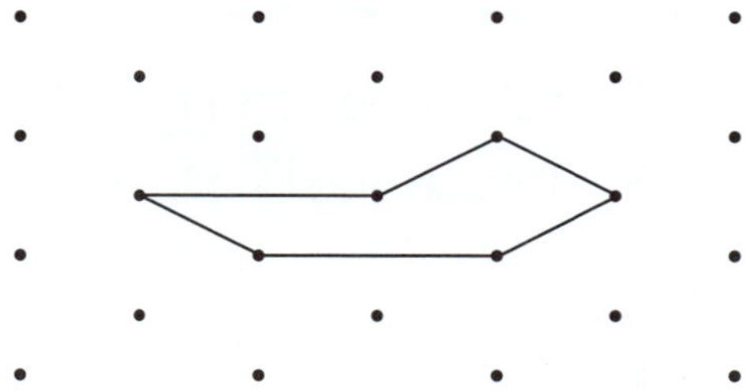

4 Millie designs a wallpaper pattern for an art competition. She shows how she designs the unit shape for her wallpaper from a square.

Millie's design:

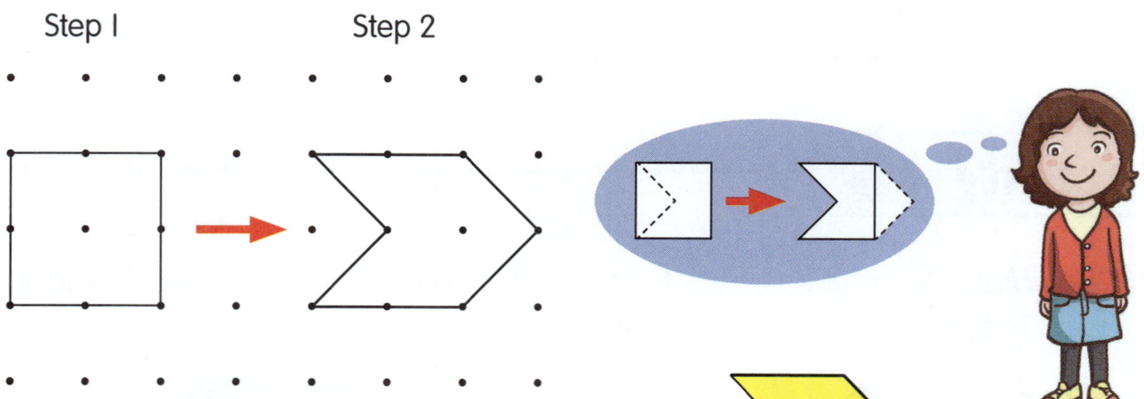

She cuts out the unit shape and makes copies of it. She colours half of the shapes blue and the other half of the shapes yellow. Then she tessellates the unit shape to make a wallpaper pattern.

Millie decides to improve her unit shape. She shows how she designs another unit shape for her wallpaper.

Millie's second design:

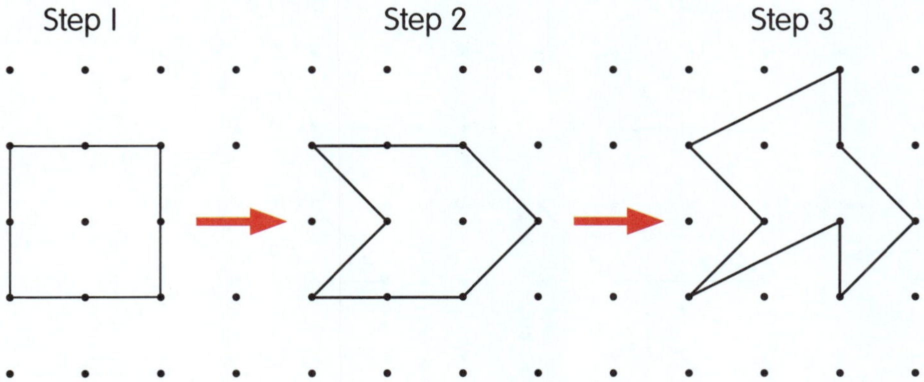

She cuts out this unit shape and makes copies of it. She colours the shapes. Then she tessellates the unit shape to make another wallpaper pattern.

Hardeep shows how he designs the unit shape for his wallpaper pattern.

Hardeep's design:

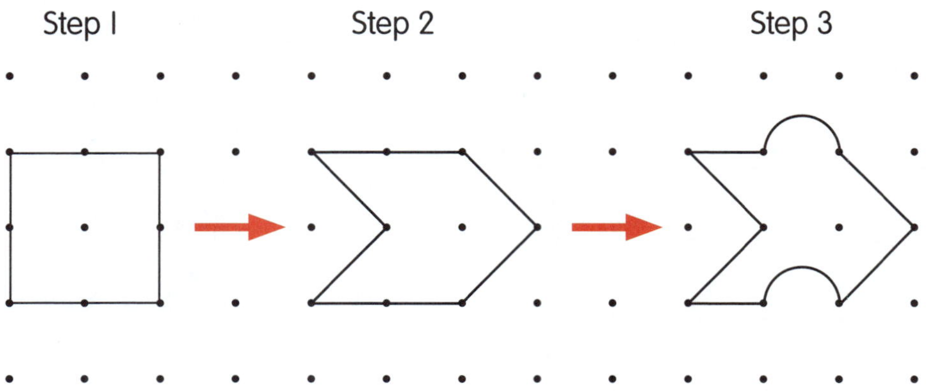

Hardeep also tessellates the unit shape to make his wallpaper pattern.

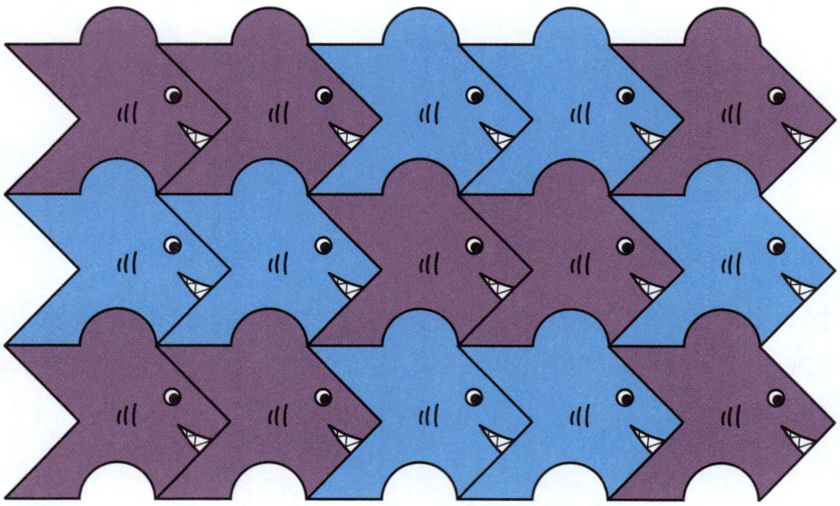

Millie and Hardeep both designed unit shapes from a square. The square can tessellate, so the new unit shapes can also tessellate.

Home Maths Encourage your child to try making some patterns that tessellate at home. Help your child to look out for unit shapes that tessellate in the world around them.

Activity

5 You will need some dotty paper. Design a unit shape that can tessellate and make your own wallpaper pattern. Start with a shape that can tessellate, such as one of the shapes below.

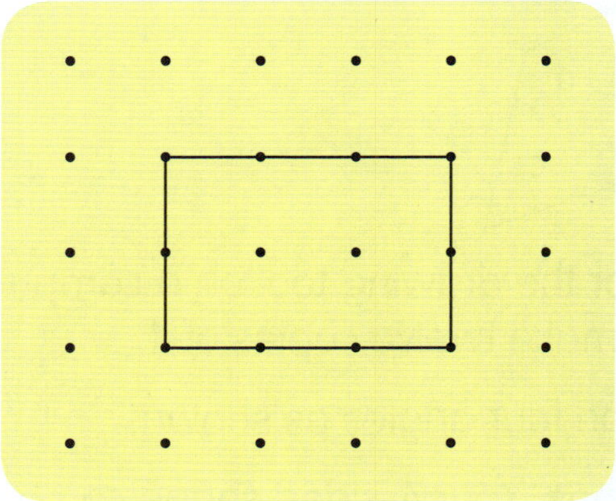

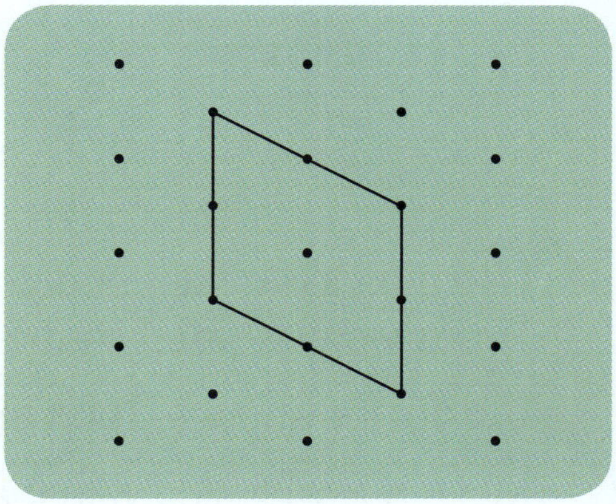

6 **Modify** each of the shapes below to design a new unit shape. Make a tessellation for each new unit shape.

a

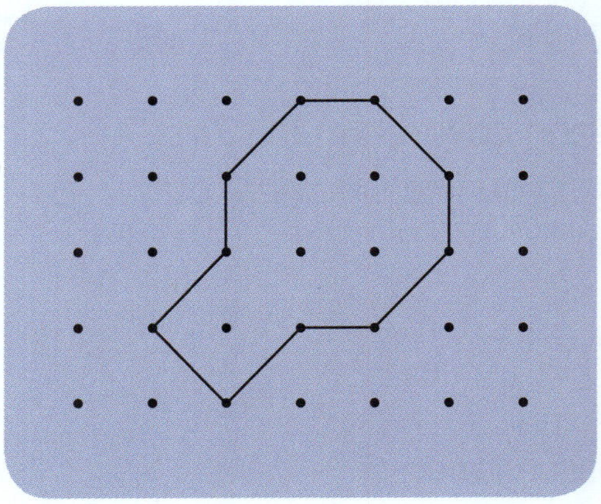

b

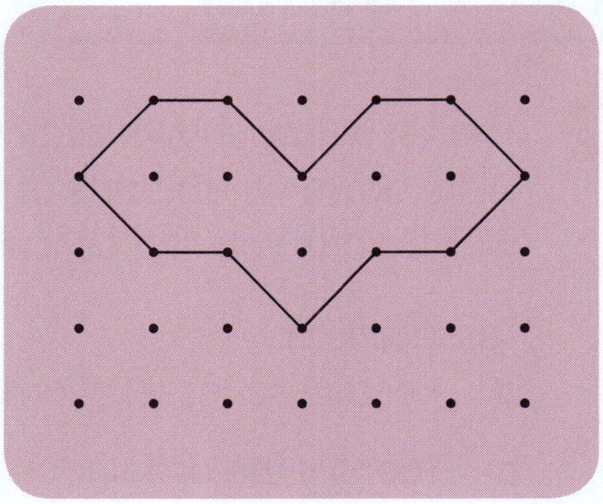

Practice Book 4B, p.123

Put On Your Thinking Caps!

7 Work in pairs.

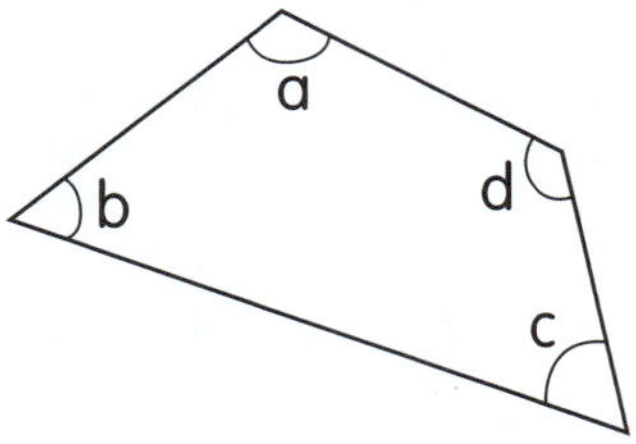

1. Use a pencil, a ruler and paper or the drawing tool on a computer to draw any 4-sided shape and make twelve copies of it.
2. Cut out the shapes. Then mark the four angles as shown.
3. Make a tessellation with the shapes. Your 4-sided shape can be different from the one shown.

Practice Book 4B, p.127

Maths Journal

8 The list below shows what has been covered in this unit. Write down which parts of this unit you like the most and which parts you find difficult.

Tessellations:

a Recognise tessellations.

b Identify the unit shape of a tessellation.

c Recognise shapes that can tessellate.

d Draw a tessellation on dotty paper for a given shape.

e Draw different tessellations for a given shape.

f Design a unit shape and make tessellations with it.